VIVAE VOCES 26

US Catholic Institutions and Immigrant Integration:
Will the Church Rise to the Challenge?

This book arises from a multi-year process led by the Center for Migration Studies of New York (CMS) and the Catholic Legal Immigration Network, Inc. (CLINIC), to engage the leaders of diverse US Catholic agencies, academics and others on immigrant integration as a potentially unifying Catholic priority. The authors wish to thank the members of the advisory group of the Catholic Immigrant Integration Initiative for lending their substantial expertise to this project, and the SC Ministry Foundation for their steadfast support for this work.

www.e-lup.com

Donald Kerwin, with Breana George

US Catholic Institutions and Immigrant Integration: Will the Church Rise to the Challenge?

Lateran
University
Press

*"Then Peter proceeded to speak and said,
'In truth, I see that God shows no partiality.'"*
Acts 10:34.

Introduction

The Catholic Church in the United States created its legendary network of cradle-to-grave institutions in response to the aspirations, needs and demands of successive generations of immigrants, their children and grandchildren (Dolan 1992, 190).[1] Like their predecessors, today's immigrants and, in particular, the second and third generation could substantially benefit from fuller participation in Catholic institutions. They could also revitalize these institutions through their strong family orientation, community-mindedness, work ethic, optimism and rich spiritual traditions.

This book argues that US Catholic institutions should renew their "special connection" to immigrants and make immigrant integration a unifying, collective priority. To do so, they will need to integrate their work more effectively and become more open and responsive to the leadership, initiative and needs of immigrants, their children and their grandchildren. They will also need to:

---

1   These institutions include parishes; elementary and high schools; universities; hospitals; mutual aid societies; service groups; charitable organizations; foundations; religious communities; fraternal, sororal and youth groups; labor ministries; Catholic media; and countless others.

- Educate Catholics on their own faith tradition and the church's identity as a church of immigrants.
- Create institutions and pastoral models that allow immigrants to sustain their cultural practices and means of religious expression.
- Reform laws and policies that impede integration, and support pro-integration policies that reflect Catholic teaching.
- Promote the good of both natives and newcomers and foster "a culture of solidarity" that crosses borders.
- Ensure that government funding does not inhibit them from addressing the structural causes of poverty and injustice.
- Honor popular religious and cultural traditions as part of a larger vision of unity through diversity.
- Retain strong ties to long-settled Catholics, but reorient Catholic institutions in light of the Church's mission to gather together God's scattered children and to serve those in need.
- Cultivate the initiative, leadership and gifts of lay persons, particularly those from immigrant communities.
- Develop creative funding strategies that substantially expand services and ministries to heavily immigrant communities.
- Revisit and rejuvenate ministries that were essential to previous generations of immigrants and their progeny.

By immigrant integration, the Catholic Church does not mean assimilation into a dominant, fixed culture. Rather, a Catholic vision of integration would locate the standard political, socio-economic, and cultural indicia of integration within a larger vision of "integral development" (development of "each" and the "whole" person) and a "union of hearts and minds" based on the universal values expressed partially and imperfectly in US and immigrant cultures (*Populorum Progressio (PP)* 14; *Quadragesimo Anno (QA)* 137). In this sense, integration represents a natural goal for an institution that understands itself as "a sacrament—that is, a sign and an instrument—of communion with God and the unity of all men" (*Lumen Gentium (LG)* 1), and that views its core services to the world as the defense of human rights and building unity "across social, political and cultural division" (*Gaudium et Spes (GS)* 42-43; Christiansen 1996, 9). Since its early days, the church has sought to unite culturally diverse and geographically distant communities through its vision of communion in Christ through the Holy Spirit (Hoover 2014, 199).

A decisive pivot towards integration would also honor the church's history and identity as a church of immigrants. At the nation's birth, Catholics constituted less than one percent of the US population and appeared poised to play only a minor role in the nation's life. Within 60 years, however, Catholics comprised the nation's largest single denomination and the church's "entire pastoral agenda ... changed to accommodate the new immigrants and their descendants" (Himes 1996). Each immigrant group had to coalesce, provide for its own and serve as its "own funder" (Matovina 2012, 90; Tomasi 1975, 182). Yet collectively a church of immigrants built a set of institutions that advanced the well-being of its members and substantially contributed to the good of the nation.[2]

The growth of Catholic institutions accelerated beginning at the end of the last era of large-scale immigration to

---

2   This book uses the word immigrant to refer to the foreign-born. The "1.5" generation refers to persons who immigrated as young children. The "second generation" refers to the US-born children of immigrants and the "third generation" to the grandchildren of immigrants.

the United States in 1920 through 1960, while the foreign-born population fell (Figure A). This growth can be attributed in part to the needs and contributions of the second, third and fourth generations. By way of contrast, between 1960 and 2010, the foreign-born population increased, but the networks of Catholic elementary schools, secondary schools and hospitals steadily contracted.[3]

Figure A. The Growth of Catholic Institutions

Year	Total Foreign Born	Archdioceses	Dioceses	Parishes	Elementary Schools	Secondary Schools	Colleges / Universities	Hospitals	Religious Brothers	Religious Sisters	Priests	Catholic Population
1850	2,244,602	4	8	1,073	----	----	30	----	----	1,941	1,081	1,606,000
1860	4,138,697	5	14	2,385	----	----	49	----	----	5,090	2,235	3,103,000
1870	5,567,229	5	21	4,396	----	----	58	----	----	11,424	3,780	3,555,000
1880	6,679,943	10	26	6,407	----	----	70	----	----	21,835	6,000	6,259,000
1890	9,249,547	10	41	7,523	----	----	89	----	----	32,534	9,168	8,909,000
1900	10,341,276	11	44	6,127	----	----	104	----	----	49,620	11,987	12,041,000
1910	13,515,886	11	50	9,017	----	----	119	451	972	70,132	17,084	16,363,000
1920	13,920,692	11	57	10,608	6,551	1,552	141	547	768	90,644	21,643	20,000,000
1930	14,204,149	13	60	12,403	7,923	2,123	166	612	2,269	111,156	27,864	20,204,000
1940	11,594,896	19	69	13,132	7,944	2,105	182	672	4,065	131,668	35,839	21,403,000
1950	10,420,908	22	79	15,533	8,589	2,189	198	760	7,620	152,178	43,889	27,766,000
1960	9,738,091	25	96	16,996	10,501	2,392	219	816	10,928	170,438	54,682	40,871,000
1970	9,619,302	29	113	18,224	9,370	1,980	232	764	10,156	153,645	58,161	47,872,000
1980	14,079,906	31	126	18,829	8,043	1,516	238	633	7,966	122,653	58,398	49,812,000
1990	19,767,316	31	141	19,559	7,291	1,296	241	641	6,835	100,334	52,126	57,019,948
2000	31,107,889	31	144	19,143	6,793	1,297	244	593	5,508	78,094	45,188	59,900,000
2010	39,916,875	37	169	18,372	5,990	1,338	232	561	4,600	56,052	39,502	68,500,000

Foreign Born Numbers Source: Gibson and Jung 2006b, Tables 3 and 4; Haines 2006a, Table Ad354-44; Haines 2006b, Table Aa1-5; 2010 American Community Survey.

Catholic Institution and Population Numbers Source: CARA 2013; Finke and Stark 1954; Johnson, Wittberg and Gautier 2014; NCES 1993, 49; P.J. Kenedy & Sons 1900-2010; Shaughnessy 1925, 189. Data not available for: number of elementary and secondary schools between the years of 1850 and 1920; hospitals and religious brothers between the years of 1850 and 1910.

---

3   The decline in Catholic elementary schools has been attributed to population shifts from cities to suburbs, costs related to aging infrastructure, rising teacher salaries, the precipitous decline in religious sisters and brothers, and diminished anti-Catholic bias (Smarick 2011, 117-18).

Despite the steady drum-beat regarding their demise, Catholic institutions may be well-positioned for another era of sustained growth, driven (again) by the growing, heavily Catholic, second and third generations, who are mostly of Latin American (primarily Mexican) and Asian descent (Figure B; Appendix A).

Figure B. United States Foreign-Born Population by Region of Origin: 1850-2010

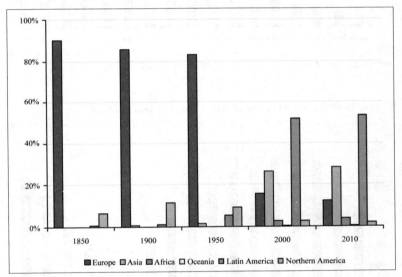

Source: Gibson and Yung 2006a; Grieco et al. 2012; Chamie 2014.

The United States is in the throes of the largest influx of immigrants in its history. Between 1970 and 2010, the US foreign-born population quadrupled from 9.6 million (4.7 percent of the population), to more than 40 million (nearly 13 percent) (Figures C and D).[4]

---

4   Unlike earlier generations, today's immigrants did not originate primarily from Europe (Appendix A).

Figure C. US Foreign-Born Population (millions): 1850-2010

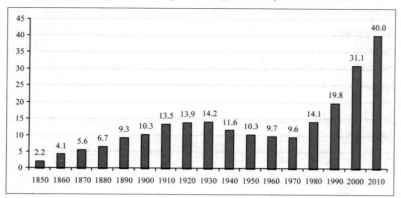

Source: Gibson and Yung 2006a; Grieco et al. 2012; Chamie 2014.

Figure D. Percent of US Population Foreign Born: 1850-2010

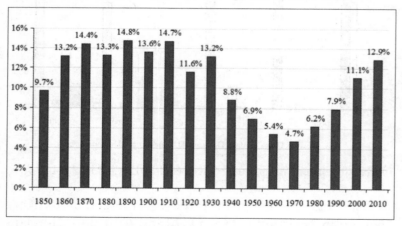

Source: Gibson and Yung 2006a; Grieco et al. 2012; Chamie 2014.

Like other wealthy and aging Western nations, the United States "will increasingly rely on young people of non-native and minority backgrounds to sustain their economic, cultural, and social vitality" (Alba and Foner 2014, S266).

12

Hispanics represent an estimated 38 percent of US Catholics; Asian, Native Hawaiian, and Pacific Islanders 4 percent; non-Hispanic black, African-American, African, and (non-Hispanic) Afro-Caribbean 3 percent (Gray et al. 2013, 9).[5] Hispanics have accounted for 71 percent of the growth in US Catholics since 1960 (Ospino 2014a, 19). They constitute 58 percent of Catholics between the ages of 18 and 34 (Millennials) and 67 percent of Millennials who regularly attend mass (Gray, Gautier and Cidade 2013). In the more racially and ethnically diverse Catholic parishes of the Southern and Western United States, the average number of infant and child baptisms far exceeds the average number of funerals (Figure E).

Figure E. Average Number of Infant/Child Baptisms and Funerals in Catholic Parishes by Region

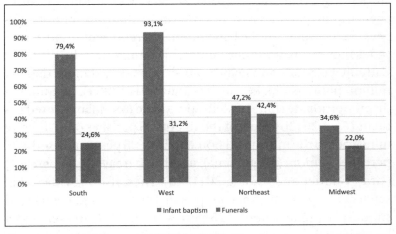

Source: Gray, Gautier and Cidade 2011, 37, 40.

---

5   This book uses the term Latino(a) and Hispanic interchangeably, tracking the language used in the studies it cites. Although it mostly discusses Latino(a) immigrants, it recognizes the substantial contributions of many other immigrant populations to the church and nation (Deck 2013, 38-40).

In recent years, scholars have questioned whether institutions that helped to integrate earlier generations of immigrants—"unions, manufacturing firms, urban schools, churches, and local political party machines"—continue to meet this need (Migration Policy Institute 2008, 15). Although the concentration of Catholic institutions reflects earlier patterns of immigration and settlement in the Northeastern and Midwestern United States (Gray, Gautier and Cidade 2011, 4-7; Smarick 2011, 117), the church's institutional infrastructure remains robust.

Catholic Charities agencies serve one in every 10 persons in poverty each year (Gautier and O'Hara 2012). More than 1.4 million students attend Catholic elementary and middle schools, and nearly 600,000 attend Catholic high schools (McDonald and Schultz 2013). Catholic colleges and universities educate 940,000 students per year (ACCU 2014). Since 1975, Catholic Charities agencies and parishes have resettled more than one million refugees. Each year, Catholic legal programs represent hundreds of thousands of low-wage and vulnerable immigrants. In 2012, 968 Catholic hospitals and health care centers served more than 93 million patients (P.J. Kennedy & Sons 2012, 2089), including a disproportionate share of Medicaid, Medicare and uninsured patients (CHA 2013b). Most of the 18,000 US parishes offer discrete ministries to the infirm and homebound (86 percent), youth (76 percent), seniors (64 percent), and the bereaved (54 percent) (Gray, Gautier and Cidade 2011, 48). They also provide social services (59 percent), sponsor parish schools (24 percent), and support regional schools (25 percent) (ibid.). Many serve as a focal point for community education and organizing initiatives. Thirty-six percent of parishes minister to discrete racial, ethnic, cultural or linguistic communities (Gray et al. 2013, 11).

Low-income immigrants, their children and grandchildren are among the groups most in need of Catholic educational, health, anti-poverty, social service and legal programs. Compared to natives, immigrants have lower education levels, college enrollment rates, incomes, homeownership rates, health insurance coverage, and English language proficiency (Motel and Patten 2013). They also struggle with higher poverty and high school drop-out rates than natives (ibid.), and are more likely to work in dangerous jobs (Kerwin 2013b). Nearly 30 percent (roughly 11.7 million) lack immigration status and fewer than one-half have become US citizens (Warren and Warren 2013; Grieco et al. 2012, 11).[6]

Immigrants could substantially benefit from greater participation in Catholic institutions. Catholic schools, for example, confer immense life and educational advantages, particularly on disadvantaged and vulnerable youth (Notre Dame Task Force 2009, 9). However, only three percent of Latino(a) children attended Catholic schools as of 2009 (ibid.).

In pursuing immigrant integration as a unifying goal, Catholic institutions would be able to rely on the leadership, talents and ambition of a record number of immigrants, nearly one-half of whom are Catholic (The Pew Forum 2008, 19), and a rapidly growing second and third generation (Matovina 2012, 222). They would also enjoy two comparative advantages based on their presence in the United States.

First, the United States enjoys a long history of successfully incorporating immigrants, even though its integration policies are mostly *ad hoc* and poorly coordinated.[7] US immigrants have

---

6   Of course, immigrants also include highly-skilled professionals, as well as a growing middle-class.
7   The United States also devotes immense resources to immigration enforcement, has failed to legalize its large unauthorized population, and sharply

traditionally benefitted from a relatively open labor market, generous family-based immigration policies, a political system that rewards participation, robust civil society institutions, and core rights that apply to persons, not just citizens, including freedom of religion, birthright citizenship and public education through high school.[8] As a result, the United States has attracted generations of immigrants who have believed that they could become and who, in fact, have been able to become Americans. A Catholic integration policy agenda should seek to conserve these shared "goods" and pre-conditions to integration.[9]

Second, religious affiliation and participation contribute to immigrant integration in the United States because of the comparative religiosity of US residents, the fact that most US immigrants are Christian (the dominant US religious tradition), and the strong foundation for acceptance of religious minorities in the US constitution and civic institutions (Foner and Alba 2008, 378-84).

A recent study analyzed whether religious affiliation and participation served as a barrier (due to discrimination) or a bridge (a source of social capital and material resources) to occupational attainment in the United States, Canada and Western Europe (Connor and Koenig 2013). It found that in the United States, attendance at Christian religious services each month increased the probability of a professional/managerial job for second generation immigrants (ibid., 29). By contrast, first-generation Western Europeans face an occupational attainment

---

distinguishes between US citizens, lawful permanent residents (LPRs), and unauthorized immigrants in the provision of public benefits.

8   Civil rights gains, the incorporation of earlier generations of immigrants, and rising rates of intermarriage have also expanded the US mainstream (Alba and Foner 2014, S279-S280).

9   It would strongly oppose, for example, attacks on birthright citizenship or efforts to disenfranchise immigrants.

"penalty" for religious affiliation, although this does not carry over to the second generation. The study concluded that in religiously pluralistic and open societies like the United States, religion contributes to occupational attainment (ibid., 31).[10]

Recent surveys of US residents on religion, immigration, national identity and culture also illustrate the growing importance of immigrants, their children and grandchildren to Catholic institutions. These findings relate primarily but not exclusively to Hispanics, the largest and among the fastest growing US ethnic groups.

This book's first chapter examines the immigrant roots of the Catholic Church in the United States. It makes the case that the defining US Catholic institutions arose in response to the needs and initiative of successive waves of immigrants, their children and grandchildren, and should be re-examined in light of their original purpose. It identifies themes and lessons from the church's work with past generations of immigrants and their descendants, which should shape and influence a unified Catholic commitment to integration. The second chapter outlines a Catholic vision of integration rooted in the concepts of "integral" human development and "communion" based on the universal values found in diverse cultures.

The third chapter describes the church's work with immigrants, paying particular attention to immigrant-led organizing

---

10   In Canada, first-generation members of minority religious groups are less likely to have a professional job than members of majority religions. The religious affiliation penalty, however, disappears when other variables (citizenship, language and time in the country) are taken into account. In addition, religious attendance in Canada is positively associated with higher occupational standing for second generation immigrants, but only for Catholics and Protestants (Connor and Koenig 2013, 30).

networks, parishes, schools, universities, the workplace, service-delivery networks, charities and health care organizations. It discusses the geographic misalignment between Catholic institutions and immigrant communities. It shows that immigrant communities need, but do not fully benefit from church institutions. It also identifies successful and promising "integration" programs and ministries, drawn from more than 60 interviews with Catholic leaders.

The fourth chapter describes the growing influence and importance of Latino(a)s and other, heavily immigrant groups to US society and to the Catholic Church, given their expanding numbers, their youth, and their overall optimism. While examining the mostly positive integration prospects for immigrants, the chapter underscores the uneven integration outcomes of different groups. It highlights the pressures faced by second- and third-generation youth and young adults in balancing multiple cultures and resisting "downward" assimilation. At the same time, it argues that the church needs to attract and prepare the second and third generations to lead Catholic institutions.

The final chapter argues that immigrant integration requires a long-term, collective commitment by Catholic institutions in partnership with government, private, and non-Catholic charitable institutions. High rates of immigration, the rapidly growing second and third generations, and the church's underlying vision of "communion" will make integration a multigenerational challenge for Catholic institutions.

I. The Past as Prologue: Historic Themes and Lessons from a Church of Immigrants

In 1789, there were 30,000 Catholics in the United States, roughly 30 priests, one newly elected bishop (John Carroll) and one fledgling university (Georgetown) (Fisher 2008, 24-5). From these humble beginnings, a national network of institutions emerged to provide integrated, cradle-to-grave services to immigrants and their progeny. As one scholar describes this history:

> With good reason American Catholicism has been called the immigrant church. The sheer number of Irish and German immigrants, followed by Italians, Poles, French Canadians, and Mexicans who entered this nation from 1820 to 1920 altered the face of American Catholicism. Once a small minority of Anglo-American landed gentry in the eighteenth century, the Catholic Church in the United States became a working class, urban Church during the nineteenth century. The entire pastoral agenda of the Church changed to accommodate the new immigrants and their descendants. (Himes 1996)

The Catholic Church's special connection to immigrants has become an article of faith and a deeply felt statement of its theological and historical identity, but one whose lessons have too often been lost or ignored. This chapter relies on several well-known historical accounts and academic literature to reveal the church's immigrant roots in the United States and to track its institutional growth, core commitments and neuralgic debates. The chapter outlines 10 themes that have shaped the church's response to immigrants and that would assume even greater salience if integration were to become a collective, unifying priority.

1. Vowed Religious Women and the Challenge of Evangelization

Vowed religious women emerge as the mostly "faceless heroes" of the Catholic Church in the United States and the driving force behind its charitable initiatives (Oates 1995, 14, 21). They established and staffed the schools, orphanages, homes for the elderly and hospitals "required by a separatist Catholic state" (Morris 1997, 179). By 1920, 224 orders and congregations of religious women administered these institutions (Brown and McKeown 1997, 87).

In 1809, Elizabeth Ann Seton, S.C. founded the first community of women religious established in the United States, the Sisters of Charity of St. Joseph, who were devoted to works of "piety, charity, and usefulness, and especially for the care of the sick, the aged, infirm, necessitous persons, and the education of young females" (Kauffman 1995, 33-34).[1] Frances Xavier Cabrini, M.S.C., founder of the Missionary Sisters of the Sacred Heart of Jesus, established 67 hospitals, schools

---

1   In 1856, Mother Seton's nephew, Bishop James Roosevelt Bayley, the first Bishop of Newark, founded the first diocesan university, Seton Hall College, in her name (Fisher 2008, 31).

and orphanages in the United States, the Americas, and Europe (Farren 1996, 81; Fisher 2008, 73-74). Mother Cabrini and Mother Seton were canonized as saints in 1946 and 1975, respectively.

In 1846, the Sisters of Mercy settled in Chicago, and founded schools, a hospital, orphan asylums and other social service programs (Dolan 1992, 324). That same year, the first Daughters of Charity arrived in Milwaukee to serve indigent immigrants, and built Milwaukee's parochial school system and its first hospital (Bouche 2012). The Daughters of Charity distinguished themselves during the cholera epidemics in 1832, 1849, and 1866, which decimated immigrant neighborhoods (Dolan 1992, 324). The School Sisters of Notre Dame arrived in the United States in 1847 and worked mainly in German parishes (ibid., 277). American sisters—many of them European immigrants—endured extraordinary hardship, poverty, peril and corruption to establish missions, schools, orphanages and other Catholic institutions that served indigenous groups, migrants and settlers in the American West (Butler 2012). By 1910, sisters administered nearly all of the nation's 400 Catholic hospitals, most of which served urban communities with large immigrant populations (McGreevy 2003, 129).

The steep decline in the number of vowed religious, particularly religious sisters—from nearly 180,000 in 1965 to 51,247 in 2013—has had dramatic implications for the staffing and financing of Catholic charitable institutions (Figure F).

Figure F. Foreign-Born Population and Catholic Vowed Religious in the United States 1850-2010

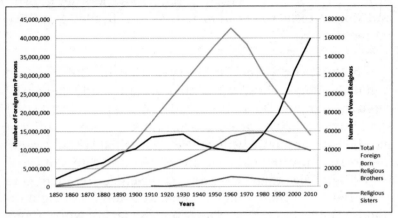

Source: Finke, Roger and Stark 1954; Johnson, Wittberg and Gautier 2014; P.J. Kenedy & Sons 1910-1940. Data for number of religious brothers between the years of 1850 and 1910 not available.

Sisters still administer hospitals, health clinics, Catholic Charities, homeless shelters, immigration programs, foundations, elementary and secondary schools and universities. To paraphrase St. Francis, they preach the Gospel, and sometimes use words. Catholic institutions will, no doubt, continue to develop new staffing and financial models, and will renew their efforts to recruit women (including from immigrant communities) to religious or consecrated life.[2] However, in the short-term, the church will not easily replace the work of women religious in evangelizing Catholics (natives and newcomers) in their own rich and challenging tradition and in educating them on *why* they should carry on this work.

---

2   Roughly one-half of dioceses with Hispanic ministry report hosting members of Latin American religious orders or communities that work with Spanish-speaking Catholics (Ospino 2014a, 26).

2. SOLIDARITY ACROSS BORDERS

The Catholic Church has always drawn heavily on its transnational identity to accompany migrants on their journeys, to cross national borders to serve immigrants, and to link sending and receiving communities. Its historic response to US immigrants exemplifies how love of neighbor "transcends the confines of national communities" (*Deus Caritas Est (DCE)* 30(a)).

Between 1790 and 1840, European priests—many of whom viewed themselves as missionaries—constituted the majority of US clergy (Fisher 2008, 29). Women religious communities in the nineteenth century overwhelmingly originated in Europe and Canada (Dolan 1992, 277). European immigrants in the nineteenth and early twentieth centuries were accompanied by priests and women religious from their communities of origin (Johnson-Mondragón 2008, 8), whose presence in Catholic institutions instilled in immigrants a sense of belonging and "homecoming" (Oates 1995; Matovina 2012, 14, 134). National parishes, which served members of distinct national, linguistic and ethnic groups, allowed generations of European immigrants, their children and grandchildren to transition into their new communities from a position of strength and acceptance (Fitzpatrick 1987, 105, 117, 155). The Hispanic parish antedated the nation's birth and the establishment of national parishes, and gave rise to popular religious traditions and practices that "functioned for Hispanics very much like language and culture" did for European immigrant communities (Ospino 2014a, 6).

Irish fraternal groups, which first appeared in the late eighteenth century, formed benevolent societies that built hospitals for the poor, cared for the sick coming off boats, and opened orphanages (Oates 1995, 25). In the late nineteenth century, European Catholic leadership began to take an increased interest in

23

the treatment of migrants in transit and in their destination communities. Port services for departing migrants were established in Hamburg, Germany, Queenstown (now Cobh, County Cork) Ireland, and Genoa, Italy, and ultimately extended and connected to reception programs in the United States. In 1887, Giovanni Batista Scalabrini, the bishop of Piacenza, Italy, founded the Missionaries of St. Charles Borromeo, to tend to the material and spiritual needs of Italian emigrants to the United States, South America and elsewhere. Immigrant institutions received significant resources from their home countries (Matovina 2012, 70).

As they do today, US Catholics responded generously to crises abroad, particularly in their communities of origin or ancestry. In 1943, the bishops founded War Relief Services, renamed Catholic Relief Services in 1955, to address the misery caused by war and natural disaster through relief and self-help initiatives (Oates 1995, 117).

Cross-border solidarity is reflected today in cooperation between migrant sending and receiving dioceses, and in Catholic initiatives to honor the "right not to have to migrate" (*EA* 65; USCC 2000, 48-51, 59). A more robust "culture of solidarity" (*Ecclesia in America (EA)* 52) could inspire development models that allow would-be migrants to flourish in their home communities. It would also maximize the contributions of expatriates and diaspora groups to their communities of birth and respond to economic, environmental and other challenges that cross national lines, including those in border communities (Kerwin 2013c).

3. HONORING CULTURE AND PRESERVING FAITH

The Catholic Church has long recognized the inter-relationship between the preservation of faith and group identity.

The religious practices and traditions of earlier generations of immigrants found a home in "national" parishes (Tomasi 1975, 2-4). Catholic schools, in turn, allowed immigrants to pass on to succeeding generations their religion, ancestral language and group symbols and identity (Gleason 1964, 160; Louie and Holdaway 2009).

Ethnic societies sought to strengthen the faith and the cultures of diverse immigrant populations in the late nineteenth century.[3] The Polish Roman Catholic Union of America was created in 1873 and, by World War I, had 100,000 members. Following the example of earlier Irish immigrants, Polish immigrants sought to retain their identity through their loyalty to the church (Fisher 2008, 71). By the last 1890s, the St. Jean Baptiste Society had more than 30,000 French-Canadian members in New England. The Central Verein, founded in 1855, linked German immigrant benevolent societies into a central mutual assistance entity. By 1916, it had 125,000 members. Between its founding in 1836 and 1908, the Ancient Order of Hibernians added nearly 130,000 members. The Knights of Columbus, established in 1882, offered life insurance and other services to its (mostly) immigrant members. By 1914, its membership had grown to more than 300,000 (Dolan 1992, 257-58).[4]

Mutual benefit societies often predated and led to the formation of national parishes like St. Stanislaus Kostka in Chicago (Dolan 1992, 181). Many Polish immigrants initially attended German-language services. Italian communities strenuously lobbied for their own parishes and for services in Italian, as opposed

---

3   Ethnic societies were similar to today's (secular) hometown associations that seek to link and support persons from the same communities of origin.

4   The Knights of Columbus now operate in 34 percent of parishes with Hispanic ministry (Ospino 2014a, 17).

to "duplex" churches which relegated them to church basements (Tomasi 1975, 117-21). The Catholic press also cemented Catholic identity and ethnic ties. Between 1830 and 1900, more than 700 Catholic newspapers appeared in print, serving every ethnic group (Dolan 1992, 258-59).

This history speaks to the need for institutions and pastoral models that allow immigrants to sustain their cultural practices and means of religious expression. While English language proficiency is often treated as an integration marker in the United States, worship in native languages has been vital to the spiritual and social well-being of generations of immigrants, among them German Catholics through the early twentieth century (Hoover 2014, 34). "As the children of God," Archbishop Thomas Wenski of Miami, Florida has said, "immigrants should feel at home in their Father's home. And the best way to feel at home is to speak in your mother's tongue." At the same time, parishes with more diverse and representative leadership conduct more ministries and programs in English, particularly for youth who are overwhelmingly US-born citizens (Ospino 2014b).

4. Immigration Policy and Immigrant Integration

Over the years, US immigration policies have greatly influenced the work of Catholic institutions. The national origins legislation of the 1920s disadvantaged (mostly Catholic) immigrants from eastern and southern European nations. The so-called *Quota Act of 1921* sought to freeze the national origin make-up of the country, setting annual limits on admission at three percent of a country's foreign-born population as of 1910.[5] The law exempted citizens from Western Hemisphere countries

5   Act of May 19, 1921, 42 Stat. 5.

from the quota. The *Immigration Act of 1924* further restricted immigration from select countries by setting the cap at two percent of the 1890 base population of national immigrant groups.[6] The 1921 and 1924 legislation slowed the growth of US Catholicism: the number of US Catholics grew only 42 percent from the mid-1920s to the mid-1950s, compared to nearly a 900 percent increase between 1830 and 1860 (Dolan 1992, 356).

The National Catholic Welfare Conference, a predecessor of the US Conference of Catholic Bishops (USCCB), opposed national origin quotas, arguing they would limit the admission of foreign-born priests and sisters who were needed to staff Catholic schools, hospitals and other charitable institutions (Scribner 2010, 4-5). The Conference also drew an explicit link between immigration policy and integration, claiming that the legislation would "retard the process of Americanization" among immigrant communities who would resent its "discriminatory nature" (ibid., 5).

Heavily Catholic Mexican immigrants have been subject to regular cycles of labor recruitment, followed by periods of nativism and large-scale deportation (Sagarena 2009, 63-64). In the current era, the massive US immigration enforcement system has divided millions of "mixed status" families, perpetuated the ill-treatment of low-wage immigrant workers and diminished cooperation between immigrant communities and the police (Kerwin 2013a, 131-36).[7] The United States spends substantially more on immigration enforcement than it collectively spends on all of its other federal law enforcement agencies and on federal and state labor standards enforcement (Meissner et al. 2013; Kerwin 2013b, 40).

---

6   Act of May 26, 1924, 43 Stat. 153.
7   A "mixed status" family is typically defined as one with a US citizen child and an unauthorized parent.

Given its size and reach, the immigration enforcement system impedes the integration of not just the 11 million US unauthorized immigrants, but also their LPR and US citizen family members. States, in turn, have pursued "attrition through enforcement" or "self-deportation" laws that seek to impoverish, evict and otherwise make integration impossible for the unauthorized and their families. Catholic institutions have directly experienced the human toll and social costs of these policies. Divided families, including those in which parental ties have been legally severed, rely heavily on Catholic institutions for support. In response to large-scale workplace raids in the mid-to-late 2000s, immigrants flocked to churches, Catholic Charities, and other safe spaces.

Full integration will require federal immigration reform and state and local laws that extend the rights and benefits of membership to all residents. At the same time, the integration process need not wait for and will not end with federal legislation. Thus, Catholic institutions have supported state and local laws that seek to regularize the lives of the unauthorized by allowing them to obtain government identification cards, driver's licenses and in-state tuition rates. Many localities have also refused to hold immigrants at the request of immigration officials.

5. Working for Justice and Practicing Charity

According to Catholic social teaching, justice should be "the aim and criterion" of political life and a core duty of "the lay faithful," but it does not obviate the human need for *caritas* (love) (*DCE* 27-28). The debate over the degree to which the Church should provide charitable services or address structural injustices is rooted in its work with earlier generations of immigrants, its intimate knowledge of the poor, and its insight into the role of social conditions in perpetuating poverty (McGreevy 2003, 130).

Founded in 1833 in France, the St. Vincent de Paul society had become established in the United States by 1845. Its goal was to learn and meet the needs of the poor and ill, to care for male orphans, and to provide spiritual counsel (Dolan 1992, 323). It also founded charitable institutions to address the needs of struggling immigrant groups, particularly youth. By the 1880s, it had become the most extensive charitable network in the church (ibid.). In 1909, it had 12,500 members and 708 "conferences" (groups of volunteers) (Oates 1995, 78-80).

By the late nineteenth and early twentieth century, Catholic priests and laity, particularly those engaged in the struggles of immigrant workers, began to argue that religious philanthropy needed to involve both charity and social reform through political engagement (Oates 1995, 55; Dolan 1992, 345; Baker 2010, 46-47). In 1910, the National Conference of Catholic Charities was founded "to wage war on the causes of poverty," including wage fraud and theft (Baker 2010, 57-58).

The "Bishops' Program of Social Reconstruction," drafted in 1919 by (then) Father John Ryan, represented a watershed moment in Catholic advocacy for social justice. The document argued for minimum wage legislation; equal wages for women; the abolition of child labor; the right to organize; health, old-age, unemployment and sickness insurance; regulation of public utility rates; worker ownership of corporate stocks; and control of monopolies (Dolan 1992, 344; Morris 1997, 151). Although this document inspired New Deal legislation, Catholic leaders rejected the growing distinction of this era between "entitlements" and public assistance, arguing that "need" created rights (Brown and McKeown 1997, 179).[8] As detailed in Chapter III, the church's integration work blends charitable services and advocacy for social justice.

6. Fidelity to Catholic Identity and Partnership with the Government

Dorothy Day, co-founder of the Catholic Worker movement, argued as early as the 1930s that the social order made charitable agencies necessary and inevitable.[9] She also sharply criticized Catholic institutions for becoming too dependent on government funding and thus beholden to government priorities (Oates 1995, 114-115). Catholic institutions rely on federal, state and local funding to an even greater degree today. Thus they must be vigilant that government partnerships do not inhibit their advocacy, limit their priorities, or lead them to neglect the spiritual dimensions of human development.

While it facilitates the integration work of church institutions, government funding also creates the risk of diminished grassroots participation in this work. In the post-World War II era, refugee resettlement resources overwhelmingly came from religiously affiliated agencies (Eby et al. 2011, 589). Since then, faith-based resettlement (and other) institutions have been "mainstreamed" and they now partner with as well as advocate before the government (Mooney 2007, 162). Partly as a result, the stated rationale for the Catholic Church's work

---

8 Catholic teaching recognizes an array of political, civic, socio-economic and cultural rights. To the Catholic Church, these rights derive from the God-given dignity of each person and give substance to, but do not exhaust the "common good" (Kerwin 2009b).

9 Day also argued that spiritual poverty inhibited communion and called for a "lonely revolution, fought out in our own hearts" (Day 1934).

with refugees has shifted from the preservation of the faith of co-religionists, to a broader human rights vision (Scribner, forthcoming).[10]

Public support for the US refugee resettlement program, and much of the program's success, can be attributed to direct community engagement with refugees. In recent years, public opposition to refugee resettlement has increased, making integration more difficult (Kerwin 2012, 8-11). Faith-based institutions—which provide extensive financial and in-kind support for refugee resettlement—nevertheless face the dilemma of how to promote integration in local communities "when resettlement now tends to be viewed by the US public as a government program" (Eby et al. 2011, 603). A related challenge is to ensure that the presence of Catholic institutions does not discourage lay initiative or lead lay persons to cede to "the professionals" responsibility for social justice and service initiatives (Hoover 2014, 182).

---

10 Scribner identifies four main reasons for the switch in the church's publicly-stated rationale for serving refugees and other migrants (Scribner, forthcoming). First, church leaders began to adopt a Cold War rationale for refugee resettlement, e.g., to prevent communist recruitment and to assist victims of communist aggression. As a result, it began to de-emphasize the Catholic character of refugees. This allowed the church to reconfigure its position in US society, as a patriotic defender of US values, rather than as a threat. Second, as Catholics became integrated into the US mainstream, religious boundaries became less stark. Third, Catholic teaching prompted the shift to a more rights-based framework for the protection of migrants, which emphasized the importance of all members of the human family, not just Catholics. Fourth, the federal government became increasingly involved in refugee resettlement. The 1948 Displaced Persons Act created a formal role for voluntary organizations ("Volags") in implementing immigration policy, and the 1980 Refugee Act established the principle of federal support for the work of Volags in serving refugees. As government contractors, Catholic agencies were required to meet government needs and standards, including the resettlement of non-Catholic populations.

The issue of government funding is part of a larger challenge on how to sustain Catholic institutions, while strengthening their mission of service to the poor and vulnerable. The beneficiaries of services represent an obvious source of support. In the mid-nineteenth century, some questioned whether Catholic hospitals were violating the spirit of Catholic charity by asking patients to pay modest fees based on their ability to pay (Oates 1995, 40). A similar debate occurred among Catholic legal immigration programs in the early 1990s. These programs overwhelmingly decided to charge modest fees, typically based on ability to pay, in order to sustain themselves and out of respect for the dignity of their clients. They found that those who paid fees tended to be more responsible and engaged clients, and valued the services more than those who received them for free.

7. Celebrating Diverse Religious Practices and Traditions

Immigrants bring a reserve of spiritual wealth to the United States and many experience their displacement, journeys and settlement in explicitly religious terms (Williams and Fortuny 2013, 170; Groody 2002; Menjívar 2003, 25, 28-29). Migration has been called a "theologizing" experience; i.e., one that can deepen the faith and increase participation in faith communities (Smith 1978; Odem 2004, 38). Many immigrants turn to religion as a source of continuity, identity and security.

The religious practices of earlier generations of European immigrants found a home in national parishes (Tomasi 1975, 2-4). By contrast, for most persons of Mexican descent in the Southwest in the nineteenth and early twentieth century, religious practice depended entirely on lay initiative (Sagarena

THE PAST AS PROLOGUE

2009, 57, 60; Dolan 1992, 176).[11] To the extent that priests served Latino(a)s, they came from different cultures (Johnson-Mondragón 2008, 8). As a result, Catholics in Northern Mexico and, after the Treaty of Guadalupe Hidalgo in 1848, in the United States developed strong traditions of lay leadership, popular religion and voluntary associations.[12] Popular religious practices remain a way to assert and transmit cultural identity (Hoover 2014, 89-90). These traditions deserve to be cultivated and honored in a church that seeks to locate and build unity based on the "universal" (Gospel) values embedded in diverse cultures.

8. Reorienting Catholic Institutions in Light of Their Mission

As US Catholics became more established and joined the middle- and upper-classes, the leaders of Catholic institutions faced a dilemma over the use of their limited human and material resources. By the mid-1960s, religious sisters began to question why they were subsidizing the education of children from affluent and middle-class families, and not working with the poor (Oates 1996, 162).[13] Lower-income Hispanics, in turn, entered a church that had become predominantly middle-class (Fitzpatrick 1990).

---

11 The first Bishop of Santa Fe, Jean Baptiste Lamy, found only 12 clergy serving 68,000 Catholics scattered across a vast swath of the nation, and mission churches in a state of neglect.

12 Under the Treaty of Guadalupe Hidalgo in 1848, Mexico ceded a territory covering all or part of eight present-day US states. The treaty allowed Mexican citizens to retain their property and to elect to become US citizens, but they nonetheless faced extraordinary discrimination. The Gadsden Purchase in 1853 covered southern Arizona and New Mexico.

13 Like the nation, Catholics fall on both ends of the socio-economic spectrum. Thirty-one percent live in families with annual incomes of less than $30,000 and 19 percent live in families with incomes of more than $100,000 (The Pew Forum 2008, 78).

A recent study of unauthorized students in three Jesuit universities concluded that "educating immigrants no longer figures as an explicit priority for many colleges and universities associated with the church, even as immigration levels have once again risen to the historic high levels found at the turn of the nineteenth century" (Schlichting et al. 2013, 8). The study laments that Jesuit universities have "[t]o some degree … lost [their] special connection with immigrants" and it applauds the recent recommitment by Jesuit university presidents to "prioritize the education of these often vulnerable and underserved students," including those without legal status (ibid., 8).

Catholic institutions need to retain their strong institutional ties to established Catholic populations, but also to remain faithful to their core mission of service to those in need. Integration can build solidarity between long-settled and newer residents through the active pursuit of shared civic and socio-economic goals. It can diminish the conflict over limited church resources by expanding opportunities, human capital and material resources to the benefit of immigrants and natives.

9. Promoting Unity and Solidarity with Immigrants

Earlier generations of Catholic immigrants faced sharp bigotry and well-organized opposition. In the mid-nineteenth to early twentieth century, nativists viewed Catholics as unpatriotic, disloyal and incapable of assimilation. Catholic institutions, particularly schools, were criticized for allegedly delaying assimilation and undermining democracy (McGreevy 2003, 45-46, 169). An 1876 cartoon by Thomas Nast depicted a swarm of bishops crawling onto US soil, their miters open like crocodile jaws waiting to devour native children, while their corrupt followers led off a weeping Lady Liberty (Morris 1997, 65-66).

Anti-Catholicism may not be so explicit today, but the dehumanizing rhetoric and scapegoating of immigrants—a large percentage of whom are Catholic—parallel attacks on Catholics from earlier periods in US history (Anti-Defamation League 2008). Moreover, fears of racial and ethnic displacement underlie immigration-related concerns and policy positions. Nearly one-fourth of Americans worry that the United States will soon become a majority minority nation (PRRI 2013, 19-20). Catholic institutions have historically taken controversial, politically pragmatic positions on immigration legislation. However, unlike in the past, they no longer present a united institutional front against repeated calumnies against their co-religionists, core tenets of Catholic teaching, or even rhetorical challenges to the tax-exempt status of Catholic entities.

10. CHANNELING LAY INITIATIVE

The historical record reveals a remarkable degree of cohesion between Catholic institutions in serving immigrants. After World War I, diocesan representatives met arriving ships, guided immigrants in their native languages through immigration processing, and helped them to secure transportation to their destinations (Morris 1997, 132). Diocesan charities, councils of lay men and women, and ethnic societies like St. Raphael's Italian Immigrant Society assisted immigrants to find housing, enrolled them in parochial or trade schools, and offered them citizenship services (Stibili 2003, 265-68).

The early decades of the twentieth century witnessed the consolidation of diverse and independent local charities under diocesan bureaus of charities and an effort to professionalize staff. These trends arose in response to new public standards for caring for the poor, state and local regulations, pressures from secular community organizations and charitable societies, and the inability of parish-based charities to address (by themselves) the problems of the immigrant poor in urban slums (Brown and McKeown 1997, 51-64; Oates 1995, 19).

In 1922, the US bishops created the National Catholic Welfare Council (NCWC) to replace the National Catholic War Council, which had been established in 1917 to coordinate US Catholic activities during World War I (Oates 1995, 95; Baker 2010, 47). In 1921, the bishops established the National Catholic School of Social Service to educate and train social workers to work in diocesan charitable bureaus (Oates 1995, 90).

At its inception, NCWC began the process of consolidating lay-administered benevolent societies under two departments, the National Council of Catholic Men and the National Council of Catholic Women (Oates 1995, 95; Baker 2010, 47). This era also saw the emergence of a national Catholic Charities umbrella agency. Like most other Catholic institutions, the Catholic Charities movement grew in response to the struggles of immigrants. During the Great Depression, Catholic Charities agencies mostly served second- and third-generation immigrants who were unemployed or under-employed (Brown and McKeown 1997, 153).

Grassroots, ethnic and lay-led institutions resisted central control, but diocesan reformers successfully argued that centralization would reduce the barriers between ethnic groups and would harmonize and professionalize services (Oates 1995, 78-81, 91). By the 1930s, the tradition of lay volunteers and participation in charitable work had significantly declined (ibid., 96-97).

The history does not argue against centralization, consistent with the dictates of subsidiary.[14] Indeed, the seamless services of Catholic institutions in the early twentieth century serve as a model for integrated services today. Yet church leaders need to develop a strategic approach to promoting lay initiative and to empowering lay leaders (particularly the second and third generations), both within existing institutions and as new Catholic institutions emerge and develop.[15] Part of the challenge requires avoiding, as a labor priest of an earlier era put it, the "awful superstition that priests alone can do the work of God" (Baker 2010, 216). The Catholic Church cannot effectively address the needs of the historically large US immigrant population without cultivating the initiative, leadership and gifts of lay persons, particularly those from immigrant communities.

---

14   Subsidiarity is a Catholic organizing principle akin to the notion of devolution. It provides that decisions should be made by the competent authorities or communities in the best position to understand and address them.

15   Lay leadership can result in more professional services and higher standards. Jesuit universities, for example, turned to lay-dominated boards partly in response to failures to meet secular accreditation standards (Morris 1997, 270-71).

II. A Catholic Vision of Integration

US Catholic institutions perform diverse functions, operate in different environments, have distinct partners, and tend to be extraordinarily active. For integration to become a unifying, collective priority, these institutions will need to embrace a common vision that is grounded in Catholic teaching, consistent with their mission, and reflective of their experience.

In creating its exhaustive network of US social and pastoral institutions, the church sought to meet the material and spiritual needs of the poor and vulnerable (Brown and McKeown 1997, 168-69), and to empower Catholics to address the underlying causes of poverty (Dolan 1992, 345). It sought to preserve the faith in response to what it viewed as the "aggressively assimilationist character of the dominant Protestant culture" (Bruce 2006, 1498; Dolan 1992, 267), and in a society that viewed Catholicism with suspicion and hostility (Kauffman 1995, 69). It sought to provide a spiritual home to persons from diverse nations and even persons from the same nation who had never viewed themselves as part of the same community (Tomasi 1975, 179-83; Alba and Orsi 2009, 36, 39). It sought to create loyal Americans who would contribute to their nation (Fitzpatrick 1987, 101), and would transform society on the basis of Catholic values (McShane 1990, 291-92; Baker 2010, 17-18). It attempted to provide immigrants and their progeny with a sense of community and with the tools they needed to live fully human lives and to serve God and neighbor, particularly those in need.[1]

The church envisions integration as a continuous, multi-generational process in which natives and newcomers work together to build communities based on the universal values found partially and imperfectly in their diverse cultures. Integration does not benefit one group at the expense of others. It draws on the gifts of all members of the community and seeks to allow all to flourish. According to the US Catholic bishops, this vision animated Catholic institutions during the nation's previous era of large-scale migration:

> A century ago, the Church responded generously to the needs of immigrants: building parishes and schools, establishing a vast array of charitable institutions, evangelizing newcomers, and being evangelized in turn by immigrant Catholics with distinctive traditions of worship and often a deep spirituality of their own. (USCC 2000, 7)

Catholic teaching does not view immigrants as a problem, but as an "an occasion that Providence gives us to help build a more just society, a more perfect democracy, a more united country, a more fraternal world and a more open and evangelical Christian community" (Pope Francis 2014). Migration, in turn, "can offer possibilities for a new evangelization, opens vistas for the growth of a new humanity foreshadowed in the

---

1   As the "labor priest" Father John Hayes (1906-2002) put it, the church teaches that human beings exist to serve God, which places their "problems on a high level; but any lower level, such as 'business is business,' is modified atheism" (Baker 2010, 34).

paschal mystery: a humanity for which every foreign country is a homeland and every homeland is a foreign country" (ibid.).

The church's vision locates the standard elements of integration—socioeconomic attainment, political participation, interaction with the host society, and a sense of belonging—within a broader vision of "integral" development, human dignity, and unity modeled on Trinitarian communion (*EA* 33). To the church, integration has never been about the full and uncritical assimilation of immigrants into a dominant culture. As discussed below, this vision of integration draws from several themes in Catholic teaching and experience.

1. SERVICE TO THE HUMAN PERSON

The public debate on immigration tends to be framed in the language of "issues" and concepts like globalization, sovereignty, security, national identity and membership. Policymakers and think-tanks speak of effective (some add "humane") migration "management" strategies. The church acknowledges the merits of these analytical frameworks, but worries that they can obscure the human beings most affected by the experience of migration; e.g., the migrants themselves, their families and their larger circles of association. Pope Benedict XVI cautioned that the "human person must always be the focal point in the vast field of international migration" (Benedict XVI 2011).

Pope Francis declared that "migrants and refugees are not pawns on the chessboard of humanity," but are "children, women and men who leave or who are forced to leave their homes for various reasons, who share a legitimate desire for knowing and having, but above all for being more" (2014). They are agents in their own lives, "rather than passive recipients of benefits or of distributions of resources and opportunities" (Ottonelli and Torresi 2013, 789). They seek better lives for themselves and their families. A Catholic vision of integration begins with the life-giving goals and aspirations of the people at the heart this phenomenon.

2. UNITY IN DIVERSITY AND EVANGELIZATION OF CULTURE

The relationship between the Catholic Church and US culture has been a source of recurrent tension. In the late nineteenth and early twentieth century, a debate flared over the degree to which Catholics should "Americanize" or assimilate into US civic institutions, traditions and values (Fisher 2008, 77; Dolan 1992, 301). The debate continues today in slightly different form over the characteristics and nature of US culture and over "what it means to be a Catholic in the United States" (Deck 2013, 47).[2]

The church views culture as the locus of the deepest values and aspirations of human beings (Fitzpatrick 1987, 25), where they build and cultivate their relationship with God and neighbor (Hoover 2014, 191). Culture "expresses, communicates and conserves ... spiritual experiences and desires that they might be of advantage to the progress of many, even of the whole human family" (GS 53). The church's vision of "unity in diversity" honors "the particularity and distinctiveness of each member" (USCCB 2012, 41). Trinitarian communion characterized by "openness to the gifts of the Spirit wherever they might appear" serves as the church's model for "unity in diversity" (USCC 2000, 55; Erga Migrantes (EM) 34; EA 33).

---

2   Some Catholics do not see a conflict between "the maintenance of strong ethnic and cultural ties *and* incorporation into American social and religious life" (Odem 2004, 47). Others take a more assimilationist position.

Catholic teaching calls upon natives and newcomers to work together to build communities based on the universal values found, in part and imperfectly, in their diverse cultures (USCC 2000). For example, the US bishops have praised Hispanic culture for its "profound faith in God, a strong sense of solidarity, an authentic Marian devotion, and a rich popular religiosity," and for valuing the human person and "relationships over tasks or possessions" (USCCB 2002, 15).

By "virtue of her mission and nature," the church "is bound to no particular form of human culture, nor to any political, economic or social system" (*GS* 42). It seeks to locate and instill universal values in (to evangelize) all cultures (*Erga migrantes (EM)* 22, 30, 34; *Evangelii Nuntiandi (EN)* 20). It rejects cultural practices that "contravene either the universal ethical values inherent in natural law or fundamental human rights" (Pope John Paul II 2001, 13). It recalls that earlier generations of immigrants were thought to be incapable of becoming full members of US society precisely because of their Catholic faith, beliefs and practices (Tomasi 1975, 47-50; Fitzpatrick 1987, 101). It worries that established, middle-class Catholics—the descendants of immigrants—have lost their prophetic distance on US culture and "have simply accepted the dominant values of American life," including "unrestrained competition for upward social and economic status and a spirit of consumerism that tends to smother human life" (Fitzpatrick 1987, 117-18). In the words of Dorothy Day, the church seeks to "change the world—make it a little simpler for people to feed, clothe, and shelter themselves as God intended them to do (Day 1946)."

Integration does not mean forcing immigrants to abandon their "language, culture, values, and traditions ... in order to be accepted" (USCC 1987, Introduction). In 2000, the US bishops decried a "kind of nativism" that emerges in the church when:

established members insist that there is just one way to worship, one set of familiar hymns, one small handful of familiar devotions, one way to organize a parish community, one language for all—and that immigrants must adapt to that way of doing things. (USCC 2000, 24)[3]

To the church, immigration does not present a problem to be solved, but an opportunity for unity. It views immigrants as instruments of evangelization. It calls on them to "witness" the Gospel in host communities through "their capacity for understanding and acceptance, their sharing of life and destiny with other people, their solidarity with the efforts of all for whatever is noble and good" (*EN* 21).[4] From its earliest days, the church has urged "aliens and sojourners" to respond to hostility with good works and, in this way, to convert members of their new communities (1 Pt 2: 11-12). It calls long-established Catholics to a "[c]onversion of mind and heart ... expressed through hospitality" (*SNL* 41). It urges Christian communities to work in unity on "bold projects aimed at changing the world by inculcating respect for the rights and needs of everyone, especially the poor, the lowly and the defenseless" (*Ut Unum Sint* 43).

3. IMMIGRANT AGENCY, COMMUNION AND SOLIDARITY

The late Monsignor George Higgins wrote that human beings do not organize themselves "merely for the sake of putting bread on the table, although this is not a bad reason for doing so," but "because of their nature as social beings" and because only through "strong and independent organizations" can they

---

3   The celebration of religious practices from home communities can represent a mark of settlement by immigrants (Fortuny and Williams 2013).

4   "Inculturation" is the two-way process that transforms culture and integrates cultural practices into Christianity.

have "a genuine say" in their communities (Higgins 1993, 185). A sense of "political efficacy" requires active "citizenship" and full participation in community life (Marks 2014, 5-6).

Guided by Catholic teaching, integration would seek to foster "authentic" and "integral development," broadly defined as "the development of each man and of the whole man" *(PP* 14) or, as a pastoral agent in the Archdiocese of Chicago put it, "not just living a better life economically, but living a full life." Integral development requires that core rights like religious liberty be honored and that each person be allowed to participate and to contribute to the common good. Moreover, it makes participation a right and a responsibility.

Central to the integration process are "the characteristics or qualities immigrants bring with them, in terms of skills, education, skin color, religion, and culture ..." (Alba and Foner 2014, S283). Institutions can facilitate, accelerate or impede integration, but they cannot make immigrants integrate. Immigrants integrate, not institutions.

Integration in the Catholic sense must also reflect the identity of immigrants as social beings. The central tenet of Catholic anthropology is that human beings develop and become fully human in relation to God and neighbor. Moreover, integration is a social process: it occurs within and between people. It requires "communion" and "solidarity."

This vision can play out very directly in Catholic institutions. A comparative study of Catholic and Evangelical churches in three cities between 1989 and 2000 found that Catholic churches emphasized building community as a way to address social problems and achieve salvation (Menjívar 2003, 34-35). By contrast, Evangelical churches stressed individual spirituality and conversion, as the way to solve the challenges of immigrant communities (ibid., 35-40).[5] Another study found that Pentecostal, Evangelical and Fundamentalist ministers in migrant-sending communities in Mexico and Guatemala did not express "any social or moral position on immigration per se, including the right to migration" (Hagan 2006, 1565).

The significant inroads made by Protestant Evangelical churches with Latino(a)s have resulted, in part, from their responsiveness to the cultural traditions and practices of discrete immigrant communities, as well as the desire of some immigrants to integrate into what they view as "a more genuine, more prosperous 'American' life" (Dias 2013). Fifty-one percent of Evangelicals who were raised Catholic report that they left the church, in part, because they "found a congregation that reaches out and helps its members more" (Pew Research Center 2014, 42).

4. THE NEED FOR ECCLESIAL INTEGRATION

Communion, the "expression of God's desire that all may be one," cannot occur unless Catholic institutions open themselves completely to the initiative and participation of immigrants (USCCB 2002, 33). Faith communities allow immigrants to build social capital, serve as a bridge to other communities, inculcate civic skills, and mobilize and guide civic participation (Foley and Hoge 2007, 11, 24). They can also be objects of activism, with organizers seeking to reform and achieve greater responsiveness from church institutions as part of a broader struggle for social justice (Odem 2004, 29).

---

5   In the interim, Evangelical communities have become far more politically active on immigration reform.

Bishop Nicholas DiMarzio of the Diocese of Brooklyn, New York has identified a list of indicators of ecclesial integration, which parallel common indicators of social integration. He sees attendance at mass and sacramental participation as an indicator of ecclesial integration, akin to labor force participation (a social indicator of integration) (DiMarzio 2014). He also analogizes attendance at English language masses to language acquisition; participation in religious education to continuance of secular education; vocations to the priesthood and religious life to military service; parish membership to naturalization; pastoral council participation to voting; personal parishes to homeownership; and inter-marriage (persons of different ethnicities) to inter-marriage (ibid.).

Additional metrics of ecclesial integration might include numbers and percentages of the second and third generation in staff and leadership positions in Catholic institutions (Ospino 2014a). Proportional Hispanic leadership has been found to lead to increased parish registration, more parental involvement in faith formation, greater parish stability and more ministries in English (Ospino 2014b). Eighty-seven of the 105 parishes in the Archdiocese of Miami, for example, have a foreign-born pastor. Immigrant leadership makes it far more likely that members of immigrant communities will view the church as a home, not a building, where both natives and newcomers move beyond a relationship of injustice or even formal equality to one based on the deeper values of solidarity, sisterhood, and love (Gerschutz 2009, 135).

5. Integration, Nationality and Membership

A vision of integration requires a corresponding vision of the kind of community (or nation) into which people will be integrating. Some states depend on an exploitable migrant labor force. They try to create the conditions that allow migrants to work productively, without them affording rights, social inclusion, or a path to membership. Most states, however, extend different levels of rights and benefits to immigrants, as they progress (or not) to citizenship (Ruhs 2013, 80-90).

Different strains of "ethno-cultural nationalism" and nativism have surfaced repeatedly in US history, including in the current era (Kerwin 2009a). At their most virulent, these movements espouse an unchanging view of US culture comprised of characteristics like religion, race, and ethnicity that newcomers either cannot or should not have to change, thus permanently excluding disfavored persons. Nativism "assumes that there is just one image of a 'real American'" (USCC 2000). It reflects the ethnocentric view rejected by Catholic teaching that particular cultures fully and exclusively express universal values (Fitzpatrick 1987, 150). It conflicts with the church's identity as a "sign and instrument of intimate union with God, and of the unity of the whole human race" (*GS* 42). It does not seek to gather, but to divide and scatter the human family.

The notion of a "creedal" nation—one based on a shared commitment to common civic values, traditions and institutions—may be the model of nationality most compatible with Catholic teaching and experience. In response to their vilification in the nineteenth century, Catholics professed their loyalty to the United States and to its commitment to religious freedom (Fitzpatrick 1987, 101). In this way, Catholics integrated by organizing around a core civic value (ibid., 102).

A vision of nationality based on shared civic values is also consistent with the church's vision of gathering together God's children based on shared belief, conviction and membership

48

in the Kingdom of God (John 11:52; Galatians 3:28). Catholic teaching on the purpose of states (to safeguard rights) and the civic responsibilities of immigrants (to participate) and receiving communities (to permit all residents to participate fully) likewise assume a generous view of state membership (Kerwin 2009a, 202-07).

The European Union (EU) has developed secular integration principles and guidelines that are consistent with Catholic teaching and might inform the church's advocacy on integration policies. The EU's "common basic principles" define integration as a "two-way process of mutual accommodation" by immigrants and natives that:

- entails respect for "basic values" of the host state;
- prioritizes education, employment, political participation, and equal access to institutions and to public and private benefits;
- requires knowledge of the host community's language, history and institutions;
- stresses the need for "frequent interaction" between immigrants and natives;
- guarantees religious liberty and respect for rights;
- mainstreams integration concerns into all government agencies and into public policy formation and implementation; and
- demands regular evaluation and policy adjustment based on clear goals, indicators and evaluation mechanisms. (European Union 2004)

III. Collective Response to Immigrants and Their Progeny

Several factors converge to position the Catholic Church to be a central "integrating" institution for immigrants: its history as a church of immigrants; the size, youth and vitality of its immigrant members; its moral teaching; and its unique understanding of integration as a process of building "communion" based on core values. This chapter identifies integration programs, ministries and models that can form the basis of a broader, "integral" response to immigrants, their children and grandchildren. These programs address barriers to integration through community building, activism, education, service provision, and pastoral services. The chapter begins by describing the church's immigrant-led community organizing work, particularly initiatives that seek to mobilize Catholic institutions in support of immigrants. It then discusses integration opportunities, challenges and promising practices in parishes, elementary schools, universities, the workplace, immigrant service networks, charities and hospitals.

1. Immigrant Leaders and Responsive Catholic Institutions

If the Catholic Church is to increase its collective response to immigrant communities, it needs to develop immigrant leaders,

51

prioritize integration needs, and mobilize its institutions accordingly. This chapter identifies national, diocesan and parish-based models for achieving these goals. In particular, it highlights immigrant-led organizing initiatives supported by the Catholic Campaign for Human Development (CCHD); the Archdiocese of Chicago's *Pastoral Migratoria*, which develops immigrant leaders who identify and pursue solutions to community challenges; parish-based organizing at Dolores Mission Church in East Los Angeles; and Centro San Juan Diego, a successful program in the Archdiocese of Denver that educates immigrants to advance in society and assume leadership roles in the church.

In each case, Catholic organizers address problems that are not typically viewed in religious terms, whether barriers to political incorporation and socio-economic attainment, or problems like alcoholism and domestic violence. Yet they view this work as part of a broader mission of "evangelization"; that is, of proclaiming God's love, "which inspires and sustains every authentic undertaking for and commitment to human liberation and advancement" (Pontifical Council for Justice and Peace 2005, 60).

i. *Catholic Campaign for Human Development*

The Catholic Campaign for Human Development (CCHD) supports community-led projects that address the underlying structures that perpetuate poverty. Since its establishment by the US bishops in 1969, CCHD has invested more than $280 million in projects to create jobs, expand affordable housing, prevent crime, increase access to public transportation, and improve schools.

Unlike other church institutions, CCHD was not created in response to the struggles of immigrants. However, its ethic of participatory democracy and empowering disadvantaged communities can be traced to community organizing campaigns in Catholic immigrant parishes beginning in the late 1930s and continuing through CCHD's inception (Engel 1998, 643-48). César Chávez, co-founder of the National Farmworkers Association (later the United Farm Workers), received one of the CCHD's initial grants (Castelli 1996, 23). CCHD also extensively supported Ernesto Cortés who founded Communities Organized for Public Service (COPS) in 1974 with six Mexican Catholic parishes in San Antonio, Texas and who later established the Texas Industrial Areas Foundation network. Lucas Benitez, executive director of the Coalition of Immokalee Workers, received CCHD's first youth leadership award. Over the years, CCHD has supported farmworker organizations, immigrant youth leadership initiatives, US-Mexico border organizing, worker centers, tenant groups, *colonia* development projects, and hundreds of other immigrant rights initiatives.

In 2001, CCHD and the Catholic Legal Immigration Network, Inc. (CLINIC) created the National Immigrant Empowerment Project, which funded 17 immigrant-led organizations over a three-year period. Many of these groups have emerged as leaders in federal and state immigration reform movements. Between 2012 and 2013, CCHD provided 20 grants to immigrant rights projects. In 2013, it awarded a $1 million dollar grant to the PICO National Network to mobilize Catholics in support of immigration reform and to CLINIC to prepare for a national legalization program.

CCHD has played a central role in the development of "institution-based community organizations" (IBCOs). IBCO organizing occurs primarily through religious congregations, but also through parent-teacher associations, faith-based organizations, labor unions and neighborhood associations (Wood, Fulton and

Partridge 2012, 11). A 2011 nationwide survey of IBCOs identified immigration as one of their priority issues, including at local, state and national levels (ibid., 19-23).

ii. *Pastoral Migratoria*

Pastoral Migratoria is a ministry of the Archdiocese of Chicago that develops immigrant leaders, identifies the needs and priorities of immigrant communities, and crafts solutions to meeting them by drawing extensively on Catholic institutions. As such, it offers an important model of how to make Catholic institutions responsive and accountable to immigrant communities. Like many Catholic immigrant-led organizing agencies, *Pastoral Migratoria* advocates in response to community needs and advances integration, but sees its work primarily in religious terms. Elena Segura, director of the Archdiocesan Office of Immigrants Affairs and Immigration Education which coordinates the program, characterizes it as an "immigrant-to-immigrant ministry ... a parish ministry of empowerment, born from the desire of immigrants to assist one another in their plight, to live their baptismal call and be agents of a broader evangelization of newcomers and natives." To Segura, the program reflects Catholic teaching on "human dignity, basic rights, family unity, and solidarity."[1]

The ministry was established in 2009 through a broad consultative process with Catholic universities, charities,

---

1   According to its mission statement, *Pastoral Migratoria* seeks to "fulfill the Church's leadership role of evangelization by welcoming immigrants, building communion between immigrants and non-immigrants as brothers and sisters in Christ, and accompanying and empowering immigrants toward their formation and integration as full members of society and people of faith in the one family of God."

parishes and community-based organizations. Prior to *Pastoral Migratoria*, Archdiocesan immigration-related education and advocacy work had been carried out under the rubric of the Catholic Campaign for Immigration Reform. *Pastoral Migratoria* has sought to form and train lay leaders, known as pastoral agents, who can address the needs of fellow immigrants in their parish communities. By early 2013, the ministry had trained 400 lay leaders, been implemented in 55 Hispanic and 11 Polish parishes with large concentrations of unauthorized immigrants, and referred more than 52,000 families to services related to labor, housing, domestic violence, and other issues. It also accompanied more than 500 Chicago area families to detention centers during the deportation of a family member and assisted 60 families of deportees with rent, health care and other needs.

At the parish level, pastoral agents form advocacy teams comprised of six to 10 people. Typically, leaders are nominated by their pastor, who in turn commits to supporting and collaborating in the work of the ministry. Leaders in different parishes form parish clusters that serve as a mechanism for mutual support, relationship building, sharing of expertise and crisis response. At the diocesan level, teams participate in quarterly forums to discuss their challenges and successes, which allow them to build relationships with other parishes and across multiple zones of the city. With a focus on relationship building within and across parishes, the ministry offers a resilient structure of lay leadership that can survive the inevitable reassignment or retirement of priests.

The model works through parishes, complements the work of priests, mobilizes lay persons, and significantly extends the church's human resources. According to the immigrant education coordinator:

The ultimate goal of any pastor is to leave something substantial behind when they move on. The goal of *Pastoral Migratoria* is to do exactly that. The relationships continue. Parishioners don't need to count on their pastor alone to carry this out; they rely on each other. That is critical as we begin to look at a church that is ever-changing, that doesn't have the same number of priests that it used to have, that focuses on lay leadership.

Pastoral agents undergo an eight-week formation training that combines reflection on the Bible and their personal experiences. The training draws heavily on the listen, learn and proclaim framework set forth by the Latin American and Caribbean bishops in their 2007 "Aparecida document," whose drafting committee was chaired by Cardinal Jorge Mario Bergoglio (CELAM 2007). It teaches pastoral agents to strengthen their capacity to observe and analyze the political, economic and social realities of their communities. It also increases their understanding of Catholic teaching, their capacities as leaders, and their role within the church and immigrant community. In addition, participants build leadership skills like public speaking, developing agendas and grassroots organizing.

To guide the formation process, a series of booklets offer reflection questions on the themes of solidarity, the dignity of work, rights, social equity, human dignity, immigration, and the baptismal call to serve. The module on immigration invites pastoral agents to reflect on such questions as: What kind of leader am I? How can I serve my community? What can I do so that the challenge of my own immigration experience can become a blessing? Through the sharing of testimonies, pastoral agents apply a spiritual framework to their own experiences. Each module opens with a liturgy that further deepens this connection.

Pastoral Migratoria is a ministry of accompaniment, a simple and powerful expression of solidarity and communion. Pastoral agents accompany parishioners as they fight isolation, poverty, and rights violations. In conjunction with spiritual formation, pastoral agents receive practical training in how to refer immigrants to appropriate social service and legal support networks. They seek to create and draw upon partnerships with Catholic, nonprofit and governmental agencies, while leveraging parishes as a source of social capital and information.[2]

In 2010, the Office for Immigrant Affairs convened a group of unauthorized youth from diocesan youth groups to form the Catholic DREAMers of Chicago.[3] These young leaders inform pastoral agents on the needs and opportunities available to unauthorized youth. Pastoral agents, in turn, disseminate this information in parishes. They have also organized parish-based Deferred Action for Childhood Arrivals (DACA) workshops at which hundreds of people have received assistance with the application process. The DACA program provides temporary relief from deportation and work authorization to certain unauthorized immigrants (DREAMers) brought to the United States as children. One of the group's leaders, Yazmin Saldivar, described the need for this work:

> My parents brought me [from Mexico] when I was three years old. I have been in Chicago since 1994. I did very well in high school and graduated with a 4.21 GPA with advanced placement courses. My teachers were very supportive, but didn't know that I was undocumented. They asked me what college I was going to

---

2   Partner institutions include Catholic Charities of the Archdiocese of Chicago; the Catholic Campaign for Immigration Reform's education and legal teams; CLINIC; the Resurrection Project; DePaul University; Dominican University; Loyola University; University of Notre Dame; ARISE Chicago; the Illinois Coalition for Immigrant and Refugee Rights; the Catholic Conference of Illinois; and the Consulate of Mexico.

3   DREAMers refer to the potential beneficiaries of the DREAM Act (Development, Relief, and Education for Alien Minors), which would provide legal status to certain persons brought to the United States as children.

and I said I didn't know. I had to tell them I was undocumented. My counselor told me I could probably go to a community college because they weren't as expensive as other colleges. When I graduated from high school in 2007, counselors didn't know how to guide undocumented students. I was ranked third in my class and my peers went to very prestigious institutions. I felt mad and frustrated. At the time, my family was not involved with the church. We were Catholic, but we would only go to mass. We weren't even aware of Catholic Charities, or the Office of Immigrant Affairs. We didn't even know that the church had a strong position on immigration. In 2006, the first marches were happening and that was the only thing we were participating in.

I continued to go to community college and I wanted to be a teacher. I got my associate's degree and went on to a four-year institution. I started taking the College of Education courses and got to the point where I needed to get a background check to get certified. I couldn't believe it. I had paid for my whole education out-of-pocket. Nobody had ever told me that I needed a background check to become a teacher. Around that time my cousins invited me to a church youth group. There is a network at the archdiocesan level that connects all of the youth groups called the *Pastoral Juvenil Hispana*. The Office of Immigrant Affairs turned to them to organize a group of DREAMers. The group coordinator knew that I was undocumented and encouraged me to become involved with the new group of Catholic DREAMers. We had the first meeting in the summer of 2010. Our first event was at Dominican University with the Cardinal to get DREAMers together and let them know we're not alone.

For Yazmin, the archdiocesan DREAMer group provides a "sense of belonging:"

After they told me I couldn't be a teacher, I was really frustrated, but God isn't going to give you a test you can't handle. That is what I communicate to the group. We have something to hold onto ... It just becomes so much easier. You can't be alone in this. There is no way you're going to make it without something greater.

Pastoral agents and Catholic DREAMers of Chicago visit predominantly non-immigrant parishes to share their testimonies. The Office for Immigrant Affairs has tapped over 100 "Immigration Parish Coordinators" in non-immigrant parishes who connect with immigrant lay leaders across the archdiocese. This network facilitates advocacy by the native-born on immigrant justice issues.

The Office for Immigrant Affairs has also created Priests for Justice for Immigrants, a network of 200 priests from more than 150 parishes who support immigrant education and advocacy. "Sisters and Brothers of Immigrants," a partner in this work, is comprised of 190 religious brothers and sisters from 59 religious orders. In 2005, Priests for Justice for Immigrants delivered 200,000 postcards in support of comprehensive immigration reform legislation to the Speaker of the House. Of these postcards, 50,000 were sent from 70 parishes with mostly native members. Such parishes also form part of an active donor base by dedicating the contributions of their congregations to the ministry.

At St. John Bosco Parish, pastoral agents have adapted their ministry to the tradition of the Salesians of Don Bosco by evoking the slogan of the beatified Argentinian of the order, Ceferino Namuncura, "*Quiero ser útil a mi gente*" ("I want to serve my community"). The pastoral agents wear T-shirts to mass with this slogan. They support parishioners in addressing educational, employment, health care, legal, housing and other needs. According to the pastoral agents, many members of the unauthorized community rely primarily on parish support.

Pastoral agents pray with and comfort families and detainees at the Broadview Detention Center on a weekly basis. They accompany persons to the consulate to obtain identification and other consular services. They provide information about immigration status for survivors of domestic violence and other crimes, and information on labor rights for those who have suffered workplace injuries. They organize Know Your Rights seminars. One parishioner paid a substantial amount of money for an immigration lawyer when there was no possibility that she could adjust to legal status. When she approached the pastoral agents to report the situation, they referred her to an attorney on a list recommended by the archdiocese. With the attorney's help, she was able to retrieve her money.

Pastoral agents also lead advocacy initiatives. For example, they organized a diocesan-wide campaign in support of the Illinois Temporary Driver's License legislation that passed in January 2013. The law makes licenses available to as many as 250,000 persons who have resided in Illinois for more than one year, are ineligible for a Social Security number, and cannot prove US legal status. In 2013, the team at St. John Bosco mobilized their parish to support immigration reform through a postcard campaign. Every family in the parish signed a postcard. The team also brought the campaign to other parishes in their deanery. Within three weeks, 40 parishes collected 50,000 postcards in support of the bill.

Pastoral Migratoria honors the agency and experience of immigrants. Reflecting on his call to serve in the ministry, one pastoral agent stated:

> There is a world of needs. What do we do to meet those needs? We have to start with ourselves, from within, to extend out to others. Our experiences as immigrants have not been for nothing. We have the best experience to be able to change people's lives.

Another pastoral agent explained:

When I heard about *Pastoral Migratoria*, immediately I felt a calling. I said this is for me. I felt that it came from my heart, from my soul. A person who doesn't have their papers will always live in fear. They don't have the confidence to go to a bank and present their consular ID, or fill out an application for an apartment. That is a humiliating experience. We are not second or third class citizens. All of us are children of God. It is unjust that they treat us with this discrimination. We feel afraid all the time, but we in the ministry have this talent. We don't let the fear overcome us. We move forward.

At the predominantly non-immigrant parish of St. Jerome, pastoral agents implemented the archdiocese's "Don't Drink and Drive" campaign. After consulting with their pastor, they launched a four-week consciousness building campaign on alcoholism through homilies and shared testimonies. While Anglo parishioners shared stories about the loss of a family member due to drunk driving, Mexican immigrants spoke to the congregation about police apprehensions as a result of drunk driving leading to significant numbers of deportations in the community. Together, the parishioners signed 2,000 faith commitment cards not to drink and drive, which included cards with the Virgin de Guadalupe. Addressing the effects of alcoholism on their communities provided a way to bridge the needs of immigrants and native-born parishioners, as well as an entry point to talk about challenges in immigrant communities.

The skills developed at the parish level, such as public speaking, enrich lay leaders' civic involvement. Some parish clusters have organized visits to congressional leaders. One pastoral agent explained:

We went to our representative's office and I wrote a speech saying that I am a small business owner and I pay taxes. I spoke of our contributions to this country. I asked him to support immigration reform.

61

The ministry also helps immigrants to relate to other integrating institutions beyond the church. Another pastoral agent reported:

> *Pastoral Migratoria* has involved me in a process of understanding the needs of my community, and the development and betterment of my community, of my neighborhood. I have learned how to consult with the alderman, and with the police. I am always there at the community meetings with police. These connections are helping me understand the options I can share with the community. The connections to Alcoholics Anonymous or domestic violence organizations expand through the parish. We're also making sure that public officials are serving our immigrant community.

The immigrant education coordinator reported that pastoral agents "advocate," "push," "question," and "organize themselves...to solve their own problems." They also strengthen the links across Catholic agencies in addressing immigrant needs. A parish cluster on the north side of Chicago worked with Catholic Charities to organize a health fair. At St. John Bosco, *Pastoral Migratoria* led to a partnership between the parish and Catholic Charities to serve survivors of domestic violence. Many pastoral agents also report that the ministry has led them to rediscover their faith. As one agent reflected:

> I am from a small town in Morelos, Mexico where bells ring at 6:00 am for mass. When you come to the United States, you lose that because you come here to work. You lose your traditions. It is a huge change. I came here in 1986, but I was going back and forth. In that process, I lost contact with my church because when I started working in the United States, I was working on Sundays and I couldn't go to mass. Many churches don't have mass each day. One loses contact with the church and with one's values from Mexico. Restoring the connection with the church once you've lost it is hard. It means entering an unknown community. The

Spanish of the priest is not the way I would like to hear it, the way he says the homily, everything is different than what you experienced previously. You have to get used to something different. It has a different taste. You get to the point where you lose contact with God completely. But arriving to an active community like this, you find that connection again. To be with families, especially because my family is separated, gives me the encouragement to find God again here.

Another pastoral agent explained:

When I came to the United States, my vision was to earn money, without regard to living life. I didn't expect to stay in the United States, but after years passed, it was impossible to return to Mexico. Ten years ago, I started going to church. It was really hard for me. After four years in the United States, I hadn't gone inside a church. I got to a point where I was better off economically, but not better off spiritually. Most of our community migrated to improve their lives, but economically, not humanly. The idea was that we would come here to have a better life, and the reality for many has been different. But for our children, life will be better. The structure of the ministry is based on immigrant needs, to provide important and practical solutions. It is perhaps the only thing in peoples' lives that allows them to focus on their human development. *Pastoral Migratoria* has helped me see the long-term possibilities. Our faith begins when we take on a different way of thinking, a different way of being.

Prior to the Senate's vote on comprehensive immigration reform legislation in June 2013, more than one thousand immigrant leaders and parishioners of the Archdiocese of Chicago marched and prayed. At a vigil presided over by Francis Cardinal George, the marchers presented 100,000 postcards from over 150 parishes that urged members of Congress to support the bill.

iii. Parish-Based Community Organizing

Dolores Mission in East Los Angeles is the poorest parish in the archdiocese. It serves the flats of Boyle Heights and is skirted by the public housing projects of Aliso Village and Pico Gardens, where more than one-half of the residents live below the federal poverty level. In the 1990s, the surrounding 16 square mile area contained 60 gangs with 10,000 members. The Jesuit ministries of Dolores Mission have worked to respond to issues of poverty and violence through a sister organization, *Proyecto Pastoral*, which develops grassroots projects in education, leadership, and service. Founded in 1986, the organization arose out of the parish's *comunidades ecclesiales de base* or Christian base communities, which are convened by lay leaders in people's homes to reflect on the Gospel in light of social conditions. *Proyecto Pastoral* now has an annual budget of $3 million and a staff of more than 50.

The organization's first project was the Dolores Mission Women's Cooperative to help women enter the workforce and obtain legal status through the *Immigration Reform and Control Act of 1986* (IRCA). Today, the cooperative runs two early childhood education centers that serve more than 100 neighborhood families. Other projects include *Camino Seguro*, a program that deploys 70 volunteers to help children walk in safety to and from the parish school in an area of high gang activity. The Guadalupe Homeless Project provides emergency shelter and meals to over 650 men annually, many of whom are immigrants, who sleep in the church and eat in the school cafeteria each morning before the students arrive. The shelter's case management and job referrals help the homeless to transition to independent living. *Proyecto Pastoral* carries out these projects in partnership with neighborhood residents who identify needs and act as agents of change.

Executive Director Cynthia Sanchez described *Proyecto Pastoral's* goals as "not to have services, but to facilitate relationships with residents to do for their community." The focus on community leadership has contributed to the parish being an incubator of other nonprofits, including Homeboy Industries, East LA Housing Coalition, and the Coalition of Humane Rights of Los Angeles (CHIRLA), which has become one of the nation's leading service-delivery, organizing and advocacy agencies for immigrants.

Father Scott Santarosa, pastor of Dolores Mission, described Christian base communities as "leaven" for understanding what is going on in people's lives and empowering them to change their own conditions. The groups provide a forum for bringing social issues to the attention of the pastor. Santarosa says: "In times of need, people come to the church. They still see the church as a place where they can get their needs taken care of. We walk with people and try to carry some of the burden."

Dolores Mission became a member of LA Voice-PICO in 2008, joining a coalition that includes 14 Catholic parishes. The parish brought significant experience advocating for immigrants at the neighborhood level and building self-help organizations to meet their needs. To initiate the parish's membership, PICO organizers engaged in 300 individual conversations with community members, which surfaced problems like lack of financial investment, low homeownership rates and division of families due to immigration enforcement. PICO then trained a local leadership team, with the support of the pastor, in power analysis and base-building organizing.

In 2012, Dolores Mission advocated for passage of the Los Angeles Responsible Banking Ordinance which requires banks to invest in local neighborhoods and businesses in order to contract with the city. During the campaign, immigrant leaders from the parish testified at city council hearings about losing their homes to foreclosure. The parish also mobilized in support of a campaign that led the Los Angeles Police Department Chief to give officers discretion to release impounded cars to unlicensed drivers without having to wait for 30 days. As a result, unauthorized immigrants can drive without the risk of losing a car to impoundment and the ensuing fees. This campaign built relationships between Jewish synagogues, African American churches, and Latino(a)s, while addressing an issue that disproportionately impacts immigrants. These organizing initiatives also allowed leaders to build relationships and skills which were needed in the national campaign for citizenship. In March 2013, 1,500 people gathered in Los Angeles for the PICO Citizenship Summit with a state senator and member of Congress. More than 400 Dolores Mission parishioners participated.

iv. *Centro San Juan Diego: Archdiocese of Denver, Colorado*

The proposed Catholic definition of integration creates a pressing challenge: how to assist immigrants to advance in US society, without assimilating into its negative features. As a practical matter, the church must develop models that allow immigrants to build their human and social capital, strengthen their faith, and participate fully in its pastoral and social life. In the late 1990s, the Archdiocese of Denver experienced a large influx of Mexican and Central American immigrants. By 2010, Hispanics represented 60 percent of Catholics in the archdiocese. Between 1998 and 2013, the number of parishes in the archdiocese with Hispanic ministry grew from eight to 52.

In 2003, the archdiocese established Centro San Juan Diego, a Hispanic institute for family and pastoral care, by merging its

Office of Hispanic Ministry with a parish-based social service organization, Bienestar Family Services. To house the center, the archdiocese invested $3 million to renovate a Catholic school building, which had been built in 1890 by Denver's first Jesuit congregation and had sat empty since its closure in 1979. The renovation took place with the support of community fund-raising, matched by grants from the Catholic Foundation of the Archdiocese of Denver and an anonymous donor. In addition, the City of Denver contributed $200,000 toward refurbishing the exterior of the building as part of its historic preservation of the downtown area. The renovation represented a substantial investment in the Hispanic community and in downtown Denver itself.

Centro San Juan Diego now serves more than 30,000 immigrants annually with the goal of "integrating Hispanics into the life of the church and society in the US." According to Luis Soto, its executive director, the center seeks "to bring Hispanics into full communion with the church in the United States," and views integration as the "condition in which we see each other as brothers and sisters with the same dignity, members of the same body of Christ, with the same responsibilities, same rights, taking part in the same church."

Centro Bienestar Family Services was founded by Sr. Alicia Cuarón in 1996 to serve the Spanish-speaking immigrant community on Denver's Westside and was housed in St. Joseph's parish prior to becoming part of Centro Juan Diego. At first, the program distributed food and clothing, but then strategically shifted from offering short-term assistance to running an adult school in order to achieve long-term impact. Through a volunteer-led nonprofit organization, the parish offered general education diploma (GED), citizenship, and English-as-a-Second Language (ESL).

At Centro San Juan Diego, about 1,000 immigrant adults are enrolled in these courses. The center also provides immigrants with the opportunity to obtain elementary and middle school certification from the Mexican Department of Education through a guided independent study program offered in cooperation with the Consulate of Denver. As an alternative to a GED, the center serves as a testing site for earning a Mexican high school diploma. Its curriculum is complemented by skills-based courses covering computer literacy, how to use public transportation, financial literacy and small business development.

The center incorporates service learning into its educational programs. It offers free tax preparation, for example, in conjunction with instruction and training for students that wish to become certified tax preparers. In 2013, seven program participants became tax return preparers registered with the Internal Revenue Service (IRS). In addition, its volunteers help more than 200 families with tax returns each year, resulting in thousands of dollars of returned income to the community. One of its tax preparers could not read or write when she came to the center. Within one year, she obtained her primary and secondary education diploma. She then completed a four-week certification course to become a tax preparer. She is now working toward a GED. "If I had not known about the center," she said, "I would still be illiterate. Now that I've graduated, I feel like a different person...Now I know that my studies will not end until an hour before death."

A state law passed in 2013 provides in-state college tuition to undocumented college students in Colorado. However, to qualify students must attend high school in the state for three years. The center educates adults who would not otherwise benefit from this law.

As the Latino(a) immigrant population in Denver became more established, the center began to offer opportunities to earn a bachelor's degree. The center partners with a private university in Puebla, Mexico to offer distance learning degree programs in fields such as business administration and information technology. Each course costs $200 and the four-year degree costs less than $10,000.

It also offers a bachelor's degree in religious studies through a partnership with a Catholic university in Mexico City. The program is geared to students who have been lay leaders in their parishes. The center augments instruction with practicum work in pastoral ministry to Spanish speakers. Its director of formation and catechesis noted that the program provides students with solid grounding in Catholic teaching and a way to apply their pastoral training in the United States.

The combination of family and pastoral services leads students to a closer relationship to the church. As its director of operations explained:

> We don't want to be known as just a social service center. It is a holistic model that includes faith formation on the pastoral side. Someone might come in for ESL, but when we start talking about other services, they reconnect with the church; we're evangelizing through the help and support we're giving them.

Conversely, participants in the Pastoral Institute take citizenship, computer, and other classes, which strengthen their pastoral work. The institute's staff underscored the need for integrated services. As one put it:

> If we want a person to improve, or try to support a person, we have to look first to their needs ... When a person first comes to the United States, they generally come without knowing any

69

English, without knowing how to find resources that could help them. They don't know how the legal system of this country works; many don't know how to use a computer ... If we can talk to them about faith, but also provide resources for them to advance in life, such as how to get a better job, how to talk to their child's teacher in English, how to use a computer so that they can obtain information such as finding work, we will do it. The underlying idea is to support a person with an integral approach. That we can serve a person based on their needs as an individual, not only as a Catholic. That is the basis of our ministry.

2. Parishes: The Core Catholic Integrating Institution

The core Catholic integrating institution is the parish. Moreover, one of the church's defining challenges has centered on parish life: how to foster the spiritual and material well-being of Catholics and to build "communion" between diverse immigrant groups and natives? To achieve this goal, the church has adopted different pastoral models.

i. *National Parishes*

The Catholic Church relied heavily on national parishes to meet the needs of past generations of immigrants (Dolan 1992, 162, 203). National parishes served distinct linguistic and ethnic groups and even people from particular regions and villages (Alba and Orsi 2009, 36, 39). Some were formally sanctioned and others effectively operated as national parishes due to the concentration of discrete immigrant groups within their boundaries (Hoover 2014, 33). National parishes have been widely credited with providing a sense of continuity, acceptance and group identity that facilitated integration into the larger society (Fitzpatrick 1987, 104). They allowed Italian immigrants, for example, who arrived with an ethnic identity limited to their own villages, to unify and compete in a pluralistic society that expected each group to act collectively and to succeed on its own (Tomasi 1975, 179-83).[4]

In the early twentieth century, national parishes fell into disfavor with many US bishops, who prioritized the establishment of pan-ethnic Catholic institutions (Hoover 2014, 8). While the national parish remains a common pastoral model for Vietnamese and Korean Catholics (Deck 2013, 42), it has mostly been supplanted by multi-cultural parishes.

Timothy Matovina refers to the "national parish dynamic" as the attempt to move from, at best, "receiving hospitality in someone else's parish to a homecoming in one's own church" (Matovina 2012, 55). The need for "one's own church" has proven particularly acute for immigrant populations that face substantial barriers to integration and acceptance (Tomasi 1975, 47-50, 178-79). A study of Notre Dame d'Haiti Catholic Church in Miami's Little Haiti, explored how a multiply-disadvantaged immigrant community—with "low levels of human capital," a significant unauthorized population, and which was targeted by harsh government policies—established "institutions and spokespersons to promote social justice" (Mooney 2007, 157).

The study found that Notre Dame d'Haiti became an effective advocacy organization due to its links to local (Catholic Charities) and national (the US bishops' conference) organizations that serve and advocate for immigrants. In addition, local church leaders created parishes and ministries that led Haitian immigrants to remain involved in the Catholic Church (Mooney

---

4   Catholic pastors still try to instill in immigrants "pan-ethnic" and group identities (Menjívar 1999, 598), and immigrants identify with broader ethnic groups with which they did not feel an affinity prior to their migration (Hoover 2014, 60).

2007, 166). It found that the "national" parish model served to "counteract" discrimination against Haitians and provided a locus for settlement, adaption, volunteer activity and organizing (167). The Pierre Toussaint Center, which was founded by Notre Dame d'Haiti, became Miami's largest social service agency and provided a "needed link" to the state and a source of government funding for the community (168-69). The state, in turn, benefited from the efficient distribution of its resources through an organization with an extensive community network.

With the exception of Haitians, African and Caribbean-born immigrants of African descent are "invisible" in many Catholic parishes and dioceses, and require targeted pastoral responses (USCCB 2008, 22-23). African immigrants earn more, are better educated and have greater English language proficiency than the foreign-born population overall. They also tend to identify with particular ethnic and national groups, and resist categorization as "African-American" or "black" which they view a threat to their identity (ibid., 21).

The national parish provided a spiritual home for generations of immigrants, unified under a diocesan structure and connected to the larger national and global entity (Fitzpatrick 1987, 108, 110). These parishes served as something of a cocoon for newcomers. Psychologists use the term "cultural encapsulation" to describe the phenomenon of socially disconnected groups that judge, identify and understand the world from their own perspective. Cultural encapsulation can cause and perpetuate ignorance regarding the perspectives of other groups or the larger society (ibid., 176). Yet it can also allow community members to build social capital and to adapt to their new situations from a position of solidarity, comfort and security (Hoover 2014, 109). The pastoral question becomes: how to sustain the national parish model or transition to new models as Catholics move, integrate into the mainstream, and identify less with their ancestral religious practices (Matovina 2012, 48)?

According to one scholar, integration occurred over three generations for the immigrants and their descendants from the last great era of immigration (roughly 1890 to 1920), with the third generation losing proficiency in their ancestral language, moving outside ethnic communities, and "taking on the characteristics of middle-class America" (Fitzpatrick 1987, 106). As ethnic identity became less pronounced and integration proceeded, loyalty to the church waned. According to the 2006 "Faith Matters" survey of 3,108 Americans, more than 40 percent of whites with Catholic parents have switched religions and nearly 45 percent rarely attend mass (Putnam and Campbell 2010, 138). Based on this experience, the church's most pressing pastoral challenge may be how to create a "home" for the second, third and subsequent generations over the next 50 years. Can the church create compelling communities for immigrants, but also make the Catholic faith more than an issue of ethnic identification? Can it honor the ethnic and cultural identities of diverse groups, while fostering a sense of communion that does not turn on class, group, ethnicity or legal status?

ii. *The Emergence of Multi-cultural Parishes*

Immigrants seek to practice their faith in communities which sustain them, whether the Catholic Church, Evangelical churches, or others. An external challenge to the Catholic Church comes from less bureaucratized, Evangelical churches that successfully incorporate the "cultural language and needs" of persons from discrete racial and ethnic groups (Menjívar 1999, 594). By way of contrast, multi-cultural parishes have emerged as an increasingly vital pastoral model in the Catholic Church.

As Figure G indicates, the number of Catholic parishes grew steadily from 1900 to 1990, while the foreign-born population fell from 1930 to 1970. The growth in Catholic parishes occurred, in part, due to the growing second and third generations. Between 1990 and 2000, the number of parishes substantially declined, while the (heavily Catholic) foreign-born more than doubled.

Figure G: Foreign-Born Population and Parishes in the United States 1850-2010

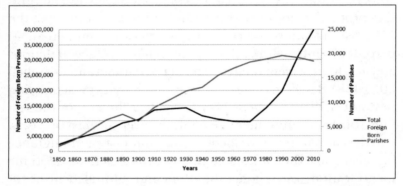

Source: Finke and Stark 1954; Johnson, Wittberg and Gautier 2014; P.J. Kenedy & Sons 1900-2010.

A 2010 survey conducted by the Center for Applied Research in the Apostolate (CARA) attributed the 7.1 percent decrease in parishes between 2000 and 2010 to misalignment between concentrations of Catholics and the location of parishes created for earlier generations of immigrants (Gray, Gautier and Cidade 2011, 4-5).[5] The report points out that since World War II Catholics have moved from cities to suburbs, and from Rustbelt communities in the Northeast and farming communities of Midwest,

---

5   The survey, to which 846 Catholic parishes (15.3 percent) responded, took place from March 2010 to December 2010.

to the Sunbelt. In addition, new immigrants have settled in large numbers across the Southern United States (ibid., 6-7). While 61 percent of parishes with Hispanic ministry are located in the West and South, 61 percent of Catholic parishes overall are located in the Northeast and Midwest (Ospino 2014a, 19).

The story of the Catholic Church in the United States in recent decades has not been one of overall decline, but of replenishment of earlier generations of immigrants (and their progeny) by new immigrants. Over the last 40 years, the number of US self-identified Catholics has grown by 75 percent to 77.7 million (Gray, Gautier and Cidade 2011, 8). Sixty to 65 percent of Latino(a)s identify themselves as Catholics (ibid., 10). However, Latino(a)s represent only 14 percent of "registered" Catholics in parishes (14 percent) (ibid., 39).

Thirty-eight percent of the CARA respondents were multi-cultural parishes, defined as those that: (1) regularly celebrate mass in other than English (or Latin); (2) have less than 40 percent non-Hispanic white parishioners; (3) meet a diversity standard (ibid., 11).[6] The South (32 percent) and West (32 percent) enjoyed the highest share of multi-cultural parishes. This model of a shared, highly diverse parish has largely supplanted the national parish model of an earlier era. The Archdiocese of Denver, for example, transformed its eight national parishes for Hispanics into multi-cultural parishes during a period of substantial growth of the Hispanic community.

The literature on ethnic ministry tends to highlight tensions between newcomers and established Catholics over use and control of parish facilities, the level of financial contributions

---

6   CARA defines parishes as diverse if the probability of randomly selected parishioners being of a different race or ethnicity is 33 percent or higher.

by established versus new members, assignment of times for mass, church decorations and ethnic celebrations (Johnson-Mondragón 2008, 8, 10; Hoover 2014, 57, 63-64). Yet multi-cultural parishes are larger and more robust than other types of parishes: on average, they have more seating capacity, registered families, registered parishioners, youth, participants in mass, and celebrations of the sacraments and rites (Gray, Gautier and Cidade 2011, 15-30, 35, 42). They also provide more social services to those in need and sponsor parochial schools at higher rates (ibid., 48, 50). They may be the harbinger of an era of sustained growth or, at least, the revitalization of Catholic parishes in response to immigrants and to the growing second and third generations. Funding, however, represents a barrier to the expansion of parishes and other institutions in communities with substantial immigrant populations. Collections at parishes with Hispanic ministry lag behind giving in parishes nationally, and collections at Spanish language masses fall far short of giving levels at other masses (Ospino 2014a, 15).

Overall, Catholics have embraced ethnic and cultural diversity. A 2011 and 2012 survey of 14,437 parishioners found that 95 percent agreed or strongly agreed that their parishes were enriched by persons from different cultural backgrounds (Ospino 2014a, 30-31).

Catholic parishes also offer extensive programs, including sacramental preparation (97 percent), religious education for children (97 percent), ministries for the infirm and homebound (86 percent), youth ministry (76 percent), ministry to seniors (64 percent), social services to meet individual needs (59 percent) and ministry to the bereaved (54 percent) (Gray, Gautier and Cidade, 2011, 48). Twenty-four percent of parishes have schools, 25 percent support regional schools (which serve multiple parishes), and 8 percent indicate a combination of both (50). Latino(a)s,

Asians and Pacific Islanders are slightly underrepresented on parish staffs in relation to the percentage of registered parishioners from these groups (55). Given that minority groups register at lower rates, the staffing disparity is certainly greater.[7]

Multi-cultural parishes appear to diminish tensions between natives and immigrants. A three-year study of Brazilian, Guatemalan and Mexican immigrants in the Atlanta metropolitan area addressed whether religious organizations mediated attitudes towards other ethnic groups.[8] It found that:

- "inter-ethnic contact at church correlated with fewer stereotypes ... and more trust of other ethnic groups";
- this effect carried over into Euro-American "attitudes toward immigrants and integration";
- church participation led parishioners to view other ethnic groups the same or more positively; and
- religious congregations play a significant role in "mediating inter-ethnic tensions," particularly for Latin American immigrants (Williams et al., n.d., 7-8).

The study concluded that the diversity of Catholics far outpaced the diversity of ministers and pastoral practices. It identified the need for parish models that honor the vision of "unity in diversity."

Several ministerial organizations have collaborated to identify models of pastoral care for immigrants and other minority groups (Johnson-Mondragón 2008, 9-12). These models fall

---

7   Pastors in parishes with Hispanic ministry report registration rates of below 50 percent for Hispanic households that attend mass (Ospino 2014a, 14).

8   The study included five focus groups in August 2008 and telephonic surveys of 714 persons between February and May 2009.

under two general categories. The "one parish, one community" model seeks to create harmony by avoiding or minimizing ministries for specific ethnic or linguistic groups. The "community of communities" model allows distinct communities *by any criteria* to form ecclesial or faith groups within traditional parishes (ibid., 9-11).

A 2007-2008 ethnographic study of the pseudonymous All Saints parish by theologian and sociologist Brett C. Hoover provides a granular analysis of a "shared parish," a term coined by Hoover to highlight the "negotiation" that occurs between distinct cultural communities that have separate masses, celebrations and ministries, but that share space and resources (Hoover 2014, 12, 57).

All Saints parish had traditionally served persons of German and Irish descent, in a majority Protestant, Midwestern city with roughly 30,000 residents. In the 1990s, the community and parish experienced a large increase in Mexican immigrants. The appointment of a Mexican priest led to the transition of All Saints from a Euro-American parish with a modest Hispanic outreach program, to a "shared parish" with Spanish language masses and ministries (57).[9]

Many longstanding members resisted sharing control of resources and leadership in a parish in which they and their families had substantially invested (21). On the other hand, the Mexican immigrant community created robust ministries, but resented their "unequal status" within the parish and the

---

9   The study identifies several factors that contribute to the transition from a "special ministry" to a shared parish: e.g., the growth of the newcomer group, the size and profile of the native group, local church politics, and the willingness of immigrants to "find a home in the parish" (19).

workplace (21). Both groups experienced a sense of displacement and insecurity (68). Against this back-drop, each focused on the "the right way" for conducting religious services, carrying out ministries and practicing the faith (69).

Intercultural negotiation on use of space, staffing, and parish procedures represented a particular challenge and source of tension (57). Feeling at a disadvantage given "asymmetrical power dynamics" in the parish and larger society, many in the Latino community avoided interaction with Euro-Americans and focused instead on strengthening group unity and safeguarding their gains and "safe space" (107, 119-123, 131). Euro-Americans, in turn, resorted to a discourse of unity, as a way to "understand their place" and rethink their identity "in a changed world" (107-108). However, they lacked a "blueprint" for achieving unity (109).

The study offers an intimate look at two culturally distinct groups operating at a linguistic and experiential divide and struggling to find a spiritual home in circumstances neither of them chose or anticipated. In short, it provides a window on the struggles and challenges of integration. It proposes "communion ecclesiology" as a more promising integration model for such parishes than assimilationist or multicultural approaches (198-200).

iii. *Parishes with Hispanic Ministry*

From 2011-2013, Boston College's School of Theology and Ministry, in partnership with CARA, undertook a national study of Catholic parishes in the United States that have "intentionally developed structures, programs, and strategies" to minister to Hispanics (Ospino 2014a, 19). The *National Study of Catholic Parishes with Hispanic Ministry* has established a database of US parishes with Hispanic ministry; sent questionnaires to pastors, directors of religious education (working with Hispanics), and parish directors of Hispanic ministry; and surveyed all diocesan directors of Hispanic ministry (7). In May 2014, Boston College released a summary report which is of the first several reports to be released on this exhaustive study.

The report begins by placing Hispanic ministry in historical context. Some Hispanic parishes antedated the creation of the United States and others became US parishes following the Treaty of Guadalupe Hidalgo in 1848 and the Gadsden Purchase in 1853. As the United States "annexed" Mexican territory, these parishes were "typically treated as 'only' national parishes" (5). During the early decades of the twentieth century, Hispanic parishes served local communities and "had few connections with each other." Later in the century, as "the policy of proliferating national parishes came under question" and Hispanic Catholics migrated to large cities, they often received pastoral care and attended mass within existing parishes, where they were "physically, pastorally, and linguistically separated." Following the Second Vatican Council, masses and faith formation in the Spanish language increased and Hispanic parishes embraced community organizing and advocacy for social justice (6). They also increasingly raised concerns related to ecclesial integration and the responsiveness of church institutions to Hispanics. A series of *Encuentros*, initiated by the US bishops in 1972, led to the development of national pastoral plan for Hispanic ministry and allowed the church to enunciate and advance its vision of unity in diversity.

The Boston College study highlights the scope, diversity and vitality of parishes with Hispanic ministry. It finds that 25 percent of the 6,269 US Catholic parishes "intentionally serve Hispanics," and 35.5 percent serve communities other than Euro-American white Catholics (8). The South is home to a disproportionate share of Hispanic ministry parishes (38 percent), but just 22 percent of all US parishes (13, 19). On average, 48 percent of the members of these parishes are Hispanic; 43 percent non-His- panic white; 4 percent Asian, Native Hawaiian or Pacific Islander; 3 percent black, African-American, or African; and one percent American Indian or Alaska Native (13-14). Seventy-two percent of Hispanic Catholics are of Mexican origin (14). Weekend mass attendance at parishes with Hispanic ministry (1,419 on aver- age) substantially exceeds the national average of 1,110. Forty- five percent offer or share responsibility for a Catholic school, compared to 33 percent of all parishes (37). Eighty percent offer adult faith formation initiatives (35), as well as other ministries, classes and service projects at high rates (16-17). The parishes provide fertile ground for political and social engagement: 43 percent reported participating in voter registration within the last year, 38 percent hosted meeting to discuss political issues, and 20 percent lobbied elected officials (17).

At the heart of the report lies a paradox of vital and growing faith communities that nonetheless lack the resources to expand and that are not sufficiently reflected in the institutional lead- ership of the church. The report concludes that while Hispanic Catholics are well-represented among permanent deacons (58 percent) and diocesan directors of Hispanic ministry (77 per- cent), they represent 10 percent of active bishops, 22 percent of pastors, 33 percent of all priests, and 42 percent of the vowed religious women engaged in Hispanic ministry (30). Moreover, Hispanics or Spanish speakers constitute less than one-half of staff at parishes with Hispanic ministry, and Hispanic parish leaders tend to belong to consultative bodies rather than "ca- nonically sanctioned parish councils." Fewer than 10 percent of Hispanic pastoral leaders view members of all "Hispanic sub- groups" as "fully integrated" participants in parish life and one in five report that these subgroups are "not all integrated" (15-17).

The study decries the low percentage of US-born Hispanic pastoral leaders in dioceses and parishes (42). It reports that communities in which Hispanics represent more than one-half of the parish population "cannot invest" in the resources to meet the growing demand for pastoral services (19). It also reports on the comparatively modest offertory collections at Spanish language masses and low parish registration rates by Hispanic households (14-15).

The study underscores the challenge and opportunity that Hispanic youth—who are overwhelmingly US-born (93 percent) and constitute the great majority of young Catholics that regularly attend mass (Gray, Cidade, and Gautier 2013)—present to the church (Ospino 2014a, 8). It also identifies multiple challenges in serving Hispanic youth that argue for a substantial commitment, including "dire socio-economic circumstances" and the "multiple demands" they face in negotiating identity in a "highly pluralistic context" (36). Yet only one in four parishes with Hispanic ministry offer "formal programs" for Hispanic youth. In addition, only 26 percent of the diocesan respondents employ a director of youth ministry for Hispanic ministry, roughly one-half of diocesan Hispanic youth ministry offices have annual budgets of less than $50,000 a year, and one in five directors works as a volunteer (28, 30).

Hispanics represent only 27 percent of the children enrolled in schools in Hispanic ministry parishes (37). Moreover, majority-Hispanic parishes are less likely to have schools (33 percent) than parishes in which Hispanics are less than one-fourth of active parishioners (60 percent). Given the relatively low levels of enrollment of Hispanic youth in Catholic schools, religious education programs assume particular importance in instructing Hispanic youth in their faith tradition (42). Nearly all parishes with Hispanic ministry offer such programs and two-thirds involve parents in these programs (33-34). Yet the report finds that the "level of investment in religious education and youth ministry programs" is "abysmally low, almost non-existent in places" (38). It concludes that lack of "appropriate investment" in Hispanic youth is "self-defeating"; proposes "serious investment" in faith formation for school-age Hispanic children that do not attend Catholic school; and recommends increased "programming and resources" for Hispanics "at risk," including gang members and prisoners (43). It argues that dioceses and parishes must "generously invest in the evangelization of Hispanic Catholics as a non-negotiable priority" (42).

iv. *St. Pius X Parish: Diocese of El Paso, Texas*

St. Pius X is a multi-cultural, bi-national parish in El Paso, Texas, situated five miles from the US-Mexico Border. The parish is distinguished by its social justice ministries, its reliance upon youth as church leaders, and its embrace of popular Catholicism (Deck 2013, 53). It seeks to develop leadership through training, formation and a ministry council (comprised of the heads of each ministry) with decision-making voice and vote.

Newcomers find a spiritual home in St. Pius X alongside border residents with whom they share cultural backgrounds and lived experience of the borderlands. Unauthorized immigrant housekeepers sit next to Border Patrol agents at mass, while homilies cover the need for immigration reform. The parish also draws parishioners from Ciudad Juárez who have settled in El Paso to escape the grisly violence in northern Mexico. The parish's lay leadership offers 63 social ministries. In the wider context of the border, parish leaders are helping to reframe the immigration debate in terms of the gifts that immigrants bring to US society and to the church.

For more than 25 years, former pastor Monsignor Arturo Bañuelas fostered an environment in which parishioners put their gifts to the service of others. He explained:

> Before Vatican II, the lay involvement was focused on helping the priest do their job. Post-Vatican II, the focus became: because of your baptism, you are consecrated and called to mission. When the people take that seriously, when they say I am consecrated, I am a missionary, I am called and I am anointed to participate in the priesthood of Jesus Christ, I am not Father's helper, but I too can make Jesus present, something happens to them and to the community. If you have a gift, then you have to look at the needs. What are the needs of the community? Our parish is a community where the gifts that the Lord gives us are called, trained, and formed, and then empowered to go and do what they are supposed to do based on the needs of this area. We have gifts, and then we respond to pastoral needs. That has worked in this parish really well. If we all pool our gifts and make Christ present in the world, then the parish continuously is transformed, reenergized. It is mission that makes us Catholics. We have to make a shift from saying I am Catholic and so I go to church, to saying I am a missionary because I am Catholic, and so I go to the world.

In 1988, Monsignor Bañuelas founded the diocesan Instituto Tepeyac which provides specialized training and formation for lay ministry. Over 25,000 lay people have since taken courses at the institute, which are offered in English and Spanish. The faculty has included over 92 instructors with doctoral degrees from Catholic universities in the United States, Mexico and Spain. At St. Pius X, 2,200 parishioners have participated in institute programs at the certificate level.

Solidarity with the poor drives the parish's response to the needs of border communities. Its ethic and pastoral challenge can be encapsulated in the phrase "*Tu eres mi otro yo*" (You are my other self) with its implication of profound inter-connectedness. It sees social justice as a pastoral concern.

The Colonia Ministry program seeks to provide hope to *colonia* residents in the midst of poverty and social inequality. The term *colonia*, which means neighborhood in Spanish, refers to an unincorporated area within 50 miles of the border that lacks basic infrastructure such as running water, sewage, electricity and paved roads. In El Paso County, an estimated 80,000 people live in 300 *colonias*.

A high concentration of *colonia* residents are immigrants who have purchased half-acre tracts on which they build houses, often in stages and with salvaged materials. Many store water in large plastic drums. When the ministry began, there was no church presence in their communities. Initially, the parish organized masses on residents' patios and began to knock on doors to network with families. The ministry sought to address the realities of *colonia* communities in partnership with their residents.

The leaders of the ministry have raised funds and contributed their professional skills in construction and administration of rural development programs. They organize clothing and food drives, Thanksgiving and Christmas dinners, and distribution of children's school supplies. The ministry has also coordinated youth groups from parishes and universities across the state in home repair projects. It is on the Red Cross disaster response list as a provider of food and relief service.

In one community, residents recently celebrated the installation of running water through a state initiative after waiting 42 years. One resident said:

> The ministry at St. Pius gave us the drive to discover what we never thought was possible. It helped us shift our mentality that

85

we would just wait for the government to eventually help us. We realized that together we could do for ourselves. They taught us about abundance; they accompanied us.

The parish's work with the poor includes support and accompaniment of community organizations, including the Centro de los Trabajadores Agrícolas Fronterizos, which is devoted to improving the working and living conditions of Mexican agricultural workers, many of whom are transported each day from El Paso to fields of New Mexico and Texas. Each year, St. Pius X holds a mass for agricultural workers close to the celebration of César Chávez's birthday, which large numbers of chile pickers attend. Carlos Marentes, the center's longtime director and a parishioner at St. Pius X, explained that the center provides shelter and food to migrant workers. However, the parish principally addresses the exploitation of migrant workers. Through this partnership, the parish, Instituto Tepeyac, and the center seek a deepened understanding of Catholic social teaching through working with migrants in the fields.

St. Pius X is the one of the few parishes in the nation with a dedicated ministry to detained unaccompanied child migrants. The Refugio Infantil Comunitario (RICO) ministry began in 2008 when parishioners collaborated with the Diocesan Migrant and Refugee Services (DMRS), a charitable legal agency for immigrants, on a proposal to offer an educational curriculum to the detained children. Each Sunday, parish volunteers visit the detention centers where children are held for up to six months. Groups of children ages 5 to 11, as well as an additional cohort of teens between the ages of 12 and 14, are also permitted to visit St. Pius X on a weekly basis to participate in prayer, song and educational activities. Many of the children come from Catholic households. They are presented to the parish at the annual immigration mass and some make their first communion during their time at St. Pius X. Receiving confession and special blessings from priests help the children to heal from the emotional trauma and abuse of their migration experience, which often includes sexual violence. In 2012, the program supported 11 pregnant girls in detention. Each year, it holds a large Thanksgiving celebration in which parish families share their holiday meal with child detainees. At Christmas, the ministry gives toys and a jacket to all children in the facilities. It also touches the lives of children in the parish school who, through the connection with child migrants, gain a profound awareness of immigration issues as part of their education.

When the ministry started, it served 70 children across three centers. As the number of border crossings by unaccompanied children and children with parents spiked in 2014, the parish served 300 children per week, proving food, shelter and assistance in reunifying with US family members.

The parish engages immigrant and second- and third-generation youth through a Spanish-speaking youth group, Grupo de Jóvenes Nazaret. The group draws between 80 and 100 participants from multiple schools and zones of the city at its weekly meetings and is the largest organized youth group in El Paso. It is led by a leadership team which develops and facilitates activities, like painting houses in *colonias*. Its weekly gatherings consist of workshop activities and structured dialogue on religious and social topics such as addiction and relationships. The group also organizes a choir with a repertoire from the *nueva canción* Latin American folk tradition.

One youth participant from Ciudad Juárez explained:

It is like finding a family. Typically, youth groups in parishes are comprised of children of families who attend church there. Here,

87

it is the opposite. The youth are drawn to the parish to participate in the group and then they bring their parents to church.

Recent immigrants turn to the group for social support on
issues related to lack of legal status and mixed-status families.
In one case, the group served as the main support for a member
whose parents had to return to Mexico for a year. The group's
annual retreat draws a few hundred participants from across the
diocese and has offered an important forum for youth who have
been personally affected by violence in Ciudad Juárez.

St. Pius X takes a collective approach to addressing immigrant needs. All of its work shares a common goal: to connect
the gifts of the church with the needs of the borderland. As Monsignor Bañuelas puts it: "We've learned how to creatively deal
with the tensions of crossing borders. It has created a harmony
of acceptance of each other's gifts."

3. Elementary Schools

The most storied Catholic institution, beyond the parish,
is the elementary school. The first Catholic schools in the New
World were "mission" schools opened by the Franciscans, Je-
suits and Ursuline sisters in Spanish and French territories,
with the goal of converting Native Americans and black slaves
(Cattaro 2002, 202). By the early nineteenth century, US bishops had begun to worry that Catholic youth would lose their
faith in the face of discrimination in common schools and
the broader society. At the Third Plenary Council of Baltimore
on December 7, 1884, the bishops resolved to "multiply" and
"perfect" Catholic schools. The Council urged pastors and parents not to "rest" until each parish had "schools adequate to
the need of its children" and it implored parents to send their

children to Catholic schools (Third Plenary Council of Baltimore 1884).

By the late nineteenth century, elementary schools had become the "principal educational institute in the Catholic community" (Dolan 1992, 262). They were established to serve poor immigrants and their children, primarily in urban centers, and sought to teach and fortify Catholic youth in the faith and educate them for citizenship (Cattaro 2002, 205). Beyond the challenges posed by discrimination and poverty, Catholic schools mostly served the progeny of European peasants, large percentages of whom were illiterate in their own language and who brought traditional "values and attitudes" that were "inimical to intellectualism" (Gleason 1964, 154-156).

The growth of Catholic schools was uneven and enrollment varied from diocese to diocese. By 1850, four-fifths of Cincinnati parishes sponsored schools which served a combined 2,000 children. In keeping with Bishop John Hughes' dictum "to build the school-house first and church afterwards," by 1865 seventy-five percent of New York City parishes sponsored schools, which served one-third (16,000) of the Catholic school age population (Dolan 1992, 263).

Yet by 1920, only 35 percent of US parishes had built schools, mostly due to financial limitations, and no more than one-third of Catholic school children ever attended them (Dolan 1992, 272, 278).[10] In addition, many Catholic school children moved to public schools following their First Communion. At the turn

---

10 A little-told story involves the number of Catholic public school children taught by Catholic women, who served as "intermediaries between immigrant families and urban public schools" (Fisher 2008, 87). Catholic lay women also played a central role in the early twentieth century in creating and staffing settlement houses for immigrants (Dolan 1992, 329).

of the century, most Catholic elementary schools offered only four or five grades (282).

Catholic high schools emerged in the mid-nineteenth century, but did not expand significantly until the first two decades of the twentieth century (292). The first "central" high school—i.e., covering multiple parishes—opened in Philadelphia in 1890. By 1912, 60,000 students were enrolled in parochial schools in Philadelphia, but only 394 attended its Catholic high school.

By 1959, there were 2,428 Catholic high schools with 810,763 students, while elementary schools served more than 4 million children (399). Researchers have identified 1964 as the high-water mark for Catholic schools, with a full 12 percent of the nation's kindergarten ("K") through 12th grade students enrolled in them (Louie and Holdaway 2009). Like parishes, the number of Catholic elementary and secondary schools grew dramatically in response to the growing second and third generations.

Figure H: Foreign-Born Population and Numbers of Catholic Schools in the United States 1850-2010

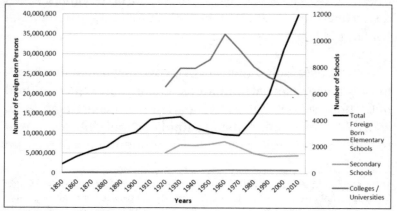

Source: NCES 1993, 49. Data for number of elementary and secondary schools between the years of 1850 and 1920 not available.

The 1950s and 1960s also witnessed the shift of many European immigrants away from center cities to suburbs, setting the stage for later parish and school closures. Between 1960 and 2010, enrollment in primary and secondary schools fell from nearly 5.3 million to 2.1 million (McDonald and Schultz 2013, 2). Schools in "older industrial cities," which had been established to serve the children of immigrants, suffered particularly high closure rates (ibid., ix). Some center city schools, however, have successfully made the transition from serving one national or dominant ethnic group, to serving newly settled multi-ethnic communities. One strategy has been to engage issues of social justice and global concerns from a faith perspective to create a receptive environment for ethnically diverse students (Cattaro 2002, 200, 208). Another successful strategy—adopted by the Archdiocese of New York—has been to assign schools to multiple parishes in order to broaden their base of support, increase enrollment, and improve the quality of instruction (Dolan 2014).

As discussed, steep declines in the numbers of vowed religious over the last 50 years have presented a stark challenge to Catholic schools. In 1940, 73,960 vowed religious—mostly sisters, but also brothers, priests and deacons—constituted more than 91 percent of total of Catholic elementary, middle and secondary school staff (McDonald and Schultz 2013, 3). By 1960, 112,029 vowed religious represented nearly 74 percent of all staff in Catholic schools. By 2013, however, 4,853 religious/clergy comprised only 3.2 percent of the staff at Catholic schools. As a result, salary costs and tuitions increased substantially (ibid., 18).

i. *The Catholic Advantage*

A rich, multi-year body of research points to the "advantages" that have accrued to generations of children educated in Catholic schools, particularly to disadvantaged students (Smarick 2011, 120-122). An analysis of US Census data from 1965 and 1966, which included information on schools attended by 28,000 persons from age six to 19, found that the percentage of former tenth grade Catholic school students that went directly to post-secondary education was 74.8 percent, compared to 54.6 percent of public school students (Morrison and Hodgkins 1971).[11]

Later research compared changes in achievement test scores by sophomores in 1980, to scores by the same set of students as seniors in 1982. It found that a previously demonstrated "Catholic school advantage" among the students had increased over two years in vocabulary, reading, math and writing (Hoffer, Greely, and Coleman 1985). Moreover, Catholic schools achieved particular success with students from minority groups, disadvantaged socioeconomic backgrounds, lower test scores and disciplinary problems. The study concluded that student background accounted for roughly one-half of the Catholic advantage, but it attributed the remaining difference to curriculum assignment policies, advanced coursework, homework, and a climate of discipline.

A more recent study analyzed survey data on 3,415 eighteen to 32 year olds in metropolitan New York, who were interviewed from 1998 to 2001 (Louie and Holdaway 2009). Nearly 30 percent of those in the study had attended Catholic schools for at least one year and 12.3 percent had graduated from or were attending Catholic schools when interviewed.

The study found that attending Catholic school for at least one year "had a positive effect on overall educational attainment,

---

11   The study accounted for differences in the student composition, social class and community setting.

even after controlling for family socioeconomic status and individual effort" (799-800). It attributed this effect to school discipline, valued relationships with school personnel, and the recognition by students that their parents had sacrificed to pay for Catholic education. It also found that Catholic school attendance (for most groups) reduced early pregnancy and arrest (for men). However, it attributed most of the difference in attainment between whites and other groups to socio-economic status, concluding that Catholic schools "did not necessarily serve as a great boost to attainment" for the low-income group.

Unlike with earlier immigrant populations, the study found that socio-economic status played a larger role than religion in determining who attended Catholic school and who could stay until graduation. Eligibility for free lunch and growing up in a one-parent home significantly reduced the likelihood of attending Catholic school. Respondents identified the quality of Catholic education, as opposed to religious or cultural reasons, as the main advantage of attending Catholic schools. For those who did not attend Catholic schools, cost proved to be a disincentive, particularly to attending secondary school.

A longitudinal, multi-phase study conducted by the Loyola Marymount University Center for Catholic Education has examined the effectiveness of Catholic schools in preparing children from low-income families in Los Angeles, California—defined as those who received tuition assistance from the archdiocesan Catholic Education Foundation (CEF)—to meet the admission requirements of state universities (Higareda et al. 2011).[12]

---

12   The Catholic Education Foundation should itself be seen an important integrating tool. It provides tuition assistance based solely on financial need to students whose parents meet federal poverty guidelines. In 2012, the median household income for a family of four required for CEF eligibility was $33,414.

The first phase of the study covered a cohort of students who received tuition assistance during the 2003-2008 academic years (24). The cohort was representative of the demographic composition of the surrounding community and public schools: ninety percent of CEF tuition assistance recipient students in the high school graduating class of 2008 were ethnic minorities. The first phase of the study revealed a 100 percent continuation rate from eighth to ninth grade in 2001 and a 98 percent graduation rate from 12th grade (after four years) for these students. It also found that 69 percent had continued their studies at Catholic high schools. By contrast, the graduation rate from all California public schools was 71 percent and was 66 percent from the public school system (the Los Angeles Unified School District (LAUSD)) in which the Catholic school students lived.

The second phase of the study replicated the findings on continuation and graduation rates with a different cohort of CEF-assisted students. It revealed a 100 percent continuation rate from eighth to ninth grade in 2004, with 64.4 percent continuing to a Catholic high school (14). More than 98 percent of tuition-assisted Catholic school students graduated from high school in four years, compared to a 69 percent graduation rate for students in California public schools and 72 percent in the LAUSD (14).

The third phase of the study, published in 2014, found similar rates of achievement among a new CEF cohort, and included comparative data on charter schools. It concluded that:

- 100 percent of tuition-assisted Catholic school students graduated from high school in 2012, compared to a graduation rate of 79 percent for California public schools and 67 percent for LAUSD schools;
- 68 percent of CEF-supported students completed the preparatory courses required by the California public

university system, compared to 37 percent of comparable public high school students and 62 percent of comparable charter school students;

- 85 percent of tuition-assisted students at Catholic high schools sat for the Scholastic Aptitude Test (SAT), compared to 40 percent at public schools, 48 percent at comparable LAUSD public schools, and 67 percent at comparable charter schools;
- tuition-assisted Catholic school students had higher SAT verbal and writing scores than students at comparable public and charter schools; and
- 96 percent of students in the CEF cohort were accepted into a two-year college or a four-year institution and 92 percent were attending college in the fall of 2012 (Huchting et al. 2014).

Students, parents, alumni, guardians, principals, and teachers interviewed for the study attributed the success of Catholic schools to a positive school culture centered on a religious, values-based mission; sense of community; high expectations; smaller schools; parental involvement; the reputation of Catholic schools for safety; and positive peer pressure (Higareda et al. 2011, 20-21; Huchting et al. 2014, 28-29).

Nationally, the Catholic high school graduation rate for 2008-09 was 99.4 percent, and 84.9 percent of 2008-09 Catholic high school graduates attended four year colleges by the fall of 2009 (Broughman, Swaim and Hryczaniuk 2011, 18, Table 13).[13] By contrast, the public high school graduation rate for

---

13   This study defines high school graduation rates as the number of 2008-09 graduates divided by the number of 12th grade students enrolled in Catholic schools around October 1, 2008 (Broughman, Swaim and Hryczaniuk 2011, A1).

2009-10 was 78.2 (Snyder and Dillow 2013, 192, Table 125),[14] and the attendance rate at four-year institutions by public high school graduates from 2006-07 was 39.5 percent in 2007-08 (ibid., 336, Table 237).

ii. *Increasing Latino(a) Enrollment*

Catholic institutions cannot integrate immigrants if they do not serve immigrants. Between 1970 and 2010-11, the percentage of ethnic minority students enrolled in Catholic schools increased from 10.8 percent to 30.2 percent (Higareda et al. 2011, 6). At the same time, however, only three percent of Latino(a) children attended Catholic schools as of 2009 (Notre Dame Task Force 2009, 11). In December 2008, Notre Dame University established a high-level Task Force on the Participation of Latino(a) Children and Families in Catholic Schools. Comprised of 52 Catholic educational and Latino(a) leaders, the Notre Dame Task Force set a goal of doubling over ten years the percentage of Latino(a) children in Catholic schools, particularly those from low-income families (11, 13). Given population growth, achieving this goal will require an increase in Latino(a) enrollment from 290,000 to more than one million students (11).

In a 2009 report, the Task Force pointed to a confluence of factors that argue for greater Hispanic enrollment in Catholic schools, including the:

- relatively poor educational outcomes of Latino(a) students in public schools;

---

14   This figure refers to averaged freshman graduate rate; that is, the percentage of students who received a high school diploma within four years of entering ninth grade (Snyder and Dillow 2013, 158).

- increased likelihood that Latino(a)s who attend Catholic schools, rather than public schools, will graduate from high school (42 percent more likely) and college (two and one-half times more likely);
- under-representation of Latino(a)s—only three percent of Latino(a) school-age children—in Catholic Schools;
- many individual Catholic schools with too few students; and
- the need to rejuvenate the Catholic school system overall (8, 26).[15]

Cost has been the most commonly identified barrier by Latino(a) parents and, indeed, by all families that wish to send their children to Catholic schools (21-22, 26). Insufficient information about Catholic schools, concerns about daycare and transportation, and lack of Spanish speaking contacts also impede Latino(a) enrollment. The Task Force argues that in order to attract Latino(a) families, the church must create culturally responsive, academically rigorous schools; provide teachers with cultural competency training; and recruit students and their families during mass and other celebrations. It also recommends the use of social networks to recruit, mentor and sponsor new families (31-34).

In the past, many of the vowed religious who administered, taught and worked in Catholic schools spoke the same language and came from the same ethnic communities as their students (29). A Task Force survey of more than 200 Catholic school principals—more than half of whom administered majority Latino(a) schools—revealed that Latino(a) teachers constitute

---

15 Since 2000, more than 1,400 Catholic schools have closed and attendance at Catholic schools has fallen by nearly 500,000. However, 300 new schools have opened.

only 34 percent of the teaching staff in urban Catholic schools with predominantly Latino(a) student bodies and that only 41 percent of the teaching staff in these schools know "any" Spanish (29-30). It recommended that Catholic schools explore new governance structures, increase lay leadership, and invest in more "well-formed" teachers, particularly Latino(a)s (38).

To many Latino(a) families, Catholic schools seem exclusive, elite and the province of other groups (39-40). Successful schools "recognize that the educational needs of their students are inseparable from the larger social need of their families and function as conduits to community resources and social services" (23).

Innovative funding strategies will be necessary to bridge the gap between the cost of tuition and fees, and what low-income families, particularly those with multiple children, can reasonably pay. They are also needed to make up the difference between Catholic school tuition which averages $3,200 for elementary school and $8,200 for high school, and the actual cost to educate students ($5,900 and $10,200 respectively) (26).

The Cristo Rey Network of Catholic high schools meets this challenge, in part, through a corporate work-study program in which students work one day per week to offset the cost of their tuition and to gain experience in the workplace. Work-study placements complement rigorous academic programs designed to prepare disadvantaged students to attend college. Other school systems depend on a combination of tuition, parental in-kind contributions, and diocesan support.

As discussed below, the Notre Dame process has inspired, guided and supported individual schools and school systems to develop plans and programs to open their schools to Latino(a) immigrants and to improve them.

iii. *Catholic Schools in East Los Angeles*

In the Boyle Heights area of East Los Angeles, the opportunity to attend a Catholic school can be a life-changing prospect. Public high schools in the area experience drop-out rates of between 40 to 60 percent, severe overcrowding, and gang activity. Santa Isabel Catholic School has a student body of 300 from K through eighth grade, an estimated 60 percent from immigrant families. Its former principal Anna Marie Silva attended the school as a child and personally experienced the benefits of a Catholic education:

> The block we lived on, most kids would end up being part of a gang. If your parents watched where you were going and who you were with, you didn't have to be the statistic. All four of the children in my family attended Santa Isabel Catholic School. The Sisters of Notre Dame founded the school on the principle of transforming the world through education and helping poor children. They helped my parents with tuition and we all went to Catholic high schools. Between the four of us, we have nine [undergraduate and advanced] degrees. I know it is because our parents partnered with the Catholic education system to do it.

To maintain high enrollment rates of immigrant families, Catholic schools in Boyle Heights have focused on addressing financial barriers and gaps in information and cultural competency. Parent ambassadors called *madrinas* (godmothers) recruit, sponsor and support immigrant parents. At the parish level, *madrinas* reach the community through religious education, youth groups, marriage encounters, and baptism. *Madrinas* also connect with parents at pre-schools, daycare centers, parks and recreation programs. According to the field consultant in Los Angeles for the University of Notre Dame's Catholic School Advantage Campaign:

If you ask any Catholic school leader what has been your most successful marketing strategy, they would say word of mouth. This
model utilizes the social capital that exists within the Latino(a)
community, and builds upon it. It really speaks to our community because it is so grassroots, and very inter-personal.

Like other schools in the area, Santa Isabel does not turn
away families away for lack of funds. It conducts individual
assessments and negotiates with families on how much they
can afford to pay. School personnel work closely with families
to apply for tuition assistance from the CEF. Schools have also
found creative solutions to helping unauthorized immigrant
parents document income earned through informal work so
that they can fulfill the requirements for receiving scholarships and financial aid. In 2012, Santa Isabel helped families to
prepare almost 200 applications to the CEF. As a result, more
than 100 students received a total of $100,000 in scholarship
support.

Santa Isabel actively encourages parents to be involved in
their children's education. To that end, it is establishing a family
literacy program that will bring parents and their pre-K children
to the school to read together. Another program allows children
to take their laptops home from school, which parents can then
use to access internet and computerized English language instruction. In addition, the staff fosters an environment in which
parents feel comfortable participating in the life of the school.
According to the former principal:

> For immigrant families, *everything* is about family. To send their
> child to a school where they don't feel a part of a family atmo-
> sphere, or where the community is not working together to raise
> that child, they already feel disconnected. If they don't speak
> English, there is a more significant barrier at public schools. Im-
> migrant families relate better to Catholic schools than public
> schools. If you come to the office of any Catholic school, the

person at the front desk will know the parents and their child's name. That family connection when living in an area where you feel lost because of language, economics or lack of education, is why I think our Catholic schools in the inner-city work so well with immigrant families.

The Notre Dame Task Force is supporting an initiative to allow Catholic schools in other parts of the nation with limited experience in serving immigrant families to learn from schools such as Santa Isabel, with the goal of adapting similar approaches in other contexts.

iv. *The Segura Educational Initiative for Children: Diocese of Richmond, Virginia*

In 2010, the Diocese of Richmond implemented the Segura Educational Initiative with the goal of providing a Catholic education to any Latino(a) child in the diocese who could not otherwise afford to attend Catholic school. The 2010 US census reported nearly a doubling of the Latino(a) population in the state of Virginia over the preceding ten years. According to its Office of Hispanic Ministry, the diocese experienced nearly a four-fold increase in registered Latino(a) parishioners between 2000 and 2010. Yet Latino(a)s represented less than 4 percent of the total student population in the 2010-2011 academic year, with virtually no recent Latino(a) arrivals enrolled.

The Segura Initiative seeks to facilitate increased Latino(a) enrollment in Catholic schools, particularly among recent immigrants and the very poor, by providing scholarships and discounted tuition. In its first year, the number of Latino(a) students enrolled in Catholic schools grew by 47 percent (from 85 to 125 students) in the city of Richmond where the program was piloted. By the 2013-14 school year, 148 Latino(a) students were enrolled through the program across the diocese. The program requires that all families make monthly tuition payments based on their income, even if only $25. To participate, families must earn at least $10,000 a year.

Parish outreach has proven the most successful way to promote Catholic schools to Latino(a) families. Many immigrant parishes lack a school. Thus, a direct invitation by pastors and diocesan formation staff to visit and learn about neighboring Catholic schools is a critical step. The Segura program's first 15 families travelled by parish bus after mass with their pastor and diocesan school administrators to a welcoming reception at All Saints Catholic School. In contrast to personal outreach, a Spanish language television commercial resulted in the enrollment of only three students.

In addition to serving in an outreach role as parent ambassadors, *madrinas* act as "school-based advocates," contributing to the retention of Latino families. Among other services, they translate communications from school and help families to complete applications for diocesan and other scholarships. They work on-site at each school for ten hours per week.

The Segura Initiative also relies heavily on the participation of parents. Second- and third-generation Latino(a) families and those with small businesses help with fundraising for scholarships. Beyond payment of at least minimal tuition, recipient parents have assisted in landscaping, painting, school maintenance, and preparation of food for school functions. Volunteer work has led to networking among immigrant parents. Most parents report that they do not participate in any civic organization other than their parish and have little knowledge of the services (if any) that are available to immigrants in their community. Some parents also participate in *convivios* or gatherings

102

organized by the Office of Hispanic Ministry that bring together Segura Initiative families from schools and parishes across the diocese. One school principal has begun to organize evening ESL classes for parents.

Gathered in a classroom at their children's school, a group of ten parents from diverse regions of Mexico, including from indigenous communities in the states of Oaxaca and Michoacán, recently spoke of how their children endured bullying, over-crowding and low academic standards in public schools. They said that the individualized attention that their children have received in Catholic school has helped them to progress rapidly. The Office of Catholic Schools reports that the test scores of the Segura Initiative cohorts have come to mirror the overall high performance of the diocesan school system.

One mother commented that the program "make[s] us feel like we're part of the community. We don't feel like foreigners. We feel more integrated and comfortable." Another parent said:

> Many Latino(a)s are Catholic, but don't have the information about Catholic school. We think you have to have a lot of money to send your kids there. Thanks to the Segura Initiative, we have that possibility. I feel closer to God and to the church now that my children attend Catholic school than before.

v. *The Accessibility of Catholic Schools to Latino(a) Families: Diocese of Brooklyn, New York*

A 2010 report on the accessibility of Catholic schools to Latino(a) families in the Diocese of Brooklyn identified several of the same themes, needs and recommendations (Kaneb, El-lison, and Florez 2010). The report was based on interviews in

2009 with 80 parents of Catholic and public school students in 10 parishes, as well as follow-up surveys.[16]

The study found that Latino(a) parents had a positive overall view of Catholic schools. They praised the schools' discipline, quality of the teachers, academic programs, respect for authority, and religious presence and instruction. Catholic school parents, in particular, stressed the values instilled by Catholic schools, their sense of family and community, and the accessibility of principals, teachers and staff. However, parents expressed concerns related to transportation to Catholic schools, special education support, limited electives, access to technology, risk of closure and limited budgets.

The report concluded that the major barrier to Latino(a) attendance at Catholic schools was the cost of tuition, uniforms, books and other fees. It found that family income, parental education, English language proficiency, and family size influenced school selection. It recommended exploring alternatives to tuition-based funding models, increasing financial assistance, and making parents aware of the availability of financial assistance and how to access it.

The study highlighted the importance of the "method" of outreach and using the right messengers to recruit Latino(a) families to Catholic schools. It recommended peer-to-peer communication, greater networking, school representatives to help Latino(a) families gain access to Catholic schools, and more Spanish-speaking teachers and staff. It also stressed the need for linguistically appropriate outreach through normal

16   Because principals of Catholic schools selected the interview and survey participants, the results may be slightly biased towards parents who are active in Catholic schools and associated parishes.

parish channels. It found that "integration" between parishes and their schools facilitated the ability to attract and reach out to public school parents in the parish community. The report recommended stressing the size, safety and family atmosphere of Catholic schools in outreach and marketing initiatives.

4. CATHOLIC COLLEGES AND UNIVERSITIES

Like elementary and secondary schools, Catholic colleges and universities were established to provide their students with the skills to advance in society and the spiritual grounding to sustain and defend the faith (Hassenger 1969, 96-97). In the mid-twentieth century, English novelist and Catholic convert Evelyn Waugh lauded US Catholic colleges for their success in improving the socio-economic standing of the laity, preserving the faith, and preparing Catholics to participate in the "'general life of the nation'" (ibid., 96).

Religious orders that administered high schools and colleges for members of their communities "backed into" creating and staffing colleges for lay students (ibid., 98). Catholic dioceses created smaller numbers of universities and the US Catholic bishops established the nation's one pontifical university, the Catholic University of America. Like other Catholic institutions, colleges arose in response to the needs of working-class immigrants and their descendants, who viewed higher education as a vehicle to employment (Gleason 1964, 157-158).

In 1955, historian Monsignor John Tracy Ellis acknowledged the success of Catholic colleges in instilling "moral virtues," but severely criticized their failure to cultivate "intellectual excellence," as measured by the formation of top scholars and intellectuals (Ellis 1955). Ellis reported that Catholic colleges produced abundant businessmen (who increasingly endowed their *alma maters*), doctors, lawyers, engineers, and government employees, but disproportionately low numbers of intellectuals. According to Ellis, Catholic colleges had succumbed to two of the worst features of secular education, "vocationalism and anti-intellectualism." He attributed this failure, in part, to the church's understandable pre-occupation with meeting the immense material and spiritual needs of the staggering number of Catholic immigrants that arrived between 1820 and 1920. Catholic intellectuals, in turn, many of them converts, received little encouragement or attention from their immigrant co-religionists, whose "all-absorbing ambition was to find a livelihood and to make the minimum necessary adjustments to their new environment" (ibid.).[17]

By the early 1960s, however, the eminent Catholic sociologist Andrew Greeley found little difference in the inclination of Catholic college graduates and graduates of other universities to enter scholarly careers and some evidence that faculty at Catholic colleges actively encouraged gifted students to pursue academic careers (Greeley 1962). Greeley suggested that this shift might be due to the "later stages of acculturation of the Catholic immigrant derived population" (Gleason 1964, 148).

For present purposes, this debate took place in the context of a broad recognition of the special relationship between Catholic colleges and heavily immigrant ethnic communities. Recent commentators, by contrast, have faulted Catholic colleges and universities for pricing out new immigrant families and failing

---

17 Other explanations for the relatively modest intellectual contributions of Catholics through the mid-twentieth century include the desire by immigrants to preserve their traditional social patterns and values from dissolution, hostility toward Catholicism in the broader society that led to a defensive intellectual posture, and the fixed teaching and positions of the Catholic Church on social issues (Gleason 1964, 150, 158, 162).

to reach out to them or even consider their needs in strategic planning (Ryscavage 2012). That said, over the last few years, Catholic colleges and universities have become more heavily engaged in the immigration reform debate. This is partly due to a growing awareness among school administrators of the effect of the US immigration system on their students. It also reflects, as Carmen Vasquez, Vice-President for Student Affairs at the University of San Diego, puts it, the way in which the immigration issue implicates core "Catholic principles on the option for the poor and vulnerable, the call to participation, community and family, and the sanctity of family."

A July 18, 2013 letter by 93 Catholic college and university presidents to Catholic members of the House of Representatives urged Congress to reform what it characterized as the "morally indefensible" immigration system. The letter underscored the history of Catholic institutions of higher education in "providing opportunities to immigrants" and stated that "no human being made in the image of God is illegal." The letter resulted from a special session at the Association of Catholic Colleges and Universities' (ACCU's) annual meeting in February 2013. The ACCU has subsequently acted as the facilitator of the overarching effort "to build collaborative networks across Catholic higher education to work toward immigration reform and best support immigrant students at Catholic colleges and universities" (ACCU 2013).

Since his retirement in 2011 as the Archbishop of Los Angeles, Roger Cardinal Mahony has partnered with ACCU to make immigration reform a priority for Catholic higher education. Mahony first held regional meetings with university presidents in Chicago, the Mid-Atlantic, the South, and the Pacific Coast sponsored by the USCCB Office of Migration and Refugee Services (MRS). At these meetings, university leaders participated in workshops on elevating awareness of immigration issues on their campuses. The ACCU, MRS and Faith in Public Life produced an immigration reform action plan for Catholic campuses that offers resources for faculty, staff and students, such as talking points for town hall forums, postcard campaigns, and op-eds.

The meetings also provided a forum for sharing practices that address the needs of immigrant students. At Villanova University and DePaul University, for example, law students assist unauthorized students to complete their applications for relief under the DACA program. At Lewis University in Chicago, a student organization called the Immigration Reform Team has developed a campus-wide Immigration Justice Pledge which commits students not to call "any human being illegal." At the University of St. Francis in nearby Joliet, Illinois, students have conducted a letter writing campaign, which urges local newspapers to abandon the term "illegal alien."

La Salle University in Philadelphia offers its Bilingual Undergraduate Studies for Collegiate Advancement (BUSCA) program to Spanish-speaking adults. Under this program, students learn English while earning an Associate's Degree. The program seeks "to empower Hispanics to be bilingual/bicultural leaders in contemporary US society."

The meetings of university presidents have led to the development of curricula on Catholic teaching, US history and immigration law. Father Daniel Groody, Associate Professor of Theology at Notre Dame University, has created modular units on immigration and the immigrant experience that can be integrated into university sociology, religious studies and other courses, and that have been widely disseminated to Catholic high schools.

The Injustice Fighting Task Force at Dominican University in River Forest, Illinois advocates for passage of the DREAM Act and to build support for unauthorized students. Dominican University President Donna Carroll has called these students "the courageous leaders of this movement" and has vowed "to stand next to them" (Dominican University 2012). The University has established a scholarship fund for unauthorized students, awards privately-funded, merit-based scholarships without regard to immigration status, and has attracted a growing individual donor base specifically dedicated to supporting unauthorized students. Overall, the university has provided $3 million in financial assistance to unauthorized students since 2010.

i. *Unauthorized Students at Jesuit Universities*

A recent study on the experience of unauthorized students at Jesuit colleges and universities found that many of these students:

- feared "exposure" during the admissions process;
- "struggled continuously" to meet tuition and other costs of college;
- could not afford the cost of room and board;
- had family obligations (like caring for siblings) which precluded their full participation in university life;
- heard hostile remarks regarding unauthorized persons from students and faculty;
- relied on "informal, *ad-hoc*" systems of support;
- could not secure necessary advice or counseling on issues relating to their legal status; and
- experienced significant stress over their reduced training, internship, and employment prospects (Schlicting et al. 2013, 11-12, 19-25).

The student respondents wanted to participate fully in the life of their university and nation, but could not. Some wondered whether they could move to Canada or work for the Society of Jesus following graduation. One student lamented, "I am always depending on someone else to provide for me" (25). Beyond the unique problems associated with lack of status, the report found that unauthorized students also faced all the challenges of first-generation college students.

The study recommended that Jesuit colleges and universities articulate the goals of access to higher education for all of their students, modify their application forms, explore creating a "common" fund to assist unauthorized students, design targeted support services and provide more effective career counseling (29-30). Sixty percent of the staff at Jesuit colleges and universities supported making education of unauthorized students an institutional priority (10). The report stressed the importance of reforming US immigration laws, which prevent young persons, who are American in every way but status, from realizing their God-given potential and participating fully in the life of their nation.

The Jesuit report aligns with the experience of Dominican University, which has found that "institutional disposition" is the key ingredient in offering unauthorized students a supportive environment. According to President Donna Carroll, four factors stand out in welcoming unauthorized students:

- when and how universities ask potential or enrolled students for their Social Security numbers;
- the structure of financial aid, with an emphasis on merit-based assistance;
- curricula and programs that recognize the existence, unique challenges and particular needs of unauthorized students; and
- the company and space to allow students to speak about their situation or not, as they see fit.

110

5. THE WORK PLACE

Migration has been called the world's oldest anti-poverty strategy (Galbraith 1979, 7). People migrate to work, whether simply to survive or (in most cases) to improve the prospects of their families. Integration occurs through the workplace and the availability and quality of work heavily determines integration outcomes. The Catholic Church's work with immigrant laborers reflects the central importance of work to the immigrant experience and the extraordinary difficulties and recurrent abuses endured by generations of low-wage immigrants. In many industries, particularly those with heavy concentrations of unauthorized workers, these conditions persist (Kerwin 2013b, 43-45), arguing for greater engagement with business leaders, employers and immigrant laborers. To guide its work, the church can draw on a remarkable body of Catholic teaching on the right to dignified work and a long commitment to workplace justice.

i. *Historic Ministry with Immigrant Laborers*

The Catholic Church's engagement on US labor issues began with the Knights of Labor, a loose confederation of "men and women of every craft, creed and color" (albeit not Asians). Founded in 1869, the Knights reached prominence in the 1880s under the leadership of Irish immigrant Terrence Powderly (Fisher 2008, 77-78; Dolan 1992, 330). By 1886, membership stood at an estimated 700,000, two-thirds of whom were Catholic. Many clerics distrusted the Knights, believing that its secret membership procedures which were developed to avoid retaliation, its initiation ceremony, and its non-sectarian identity represented a threat to the church and its influence on Catholic members (McGreevy 2003, 131-132; Dolan 1992, 330-331).

111

In 1887, fearful that the Vatican would forbid US Catholics from joining the Knights, Cardinal James Gibbons of Baltimore presented a document to Vatican officials on behalf of a core of US bishops that defended the right to organize, raised the specter of estrangement of the Catholic working class from the church, and urged that the Knights not be condemned (Dolan 1992, 332-333). The Vatican ultimately lifted its ban on the Knights (which had applied in Canada and arguably elsewhere), provided that the Knights cull references from its constitution that seemed "to savor of socialism and communism" (Dolan 1992, 333). According to Monsignor George Higgins, Gibbons' intervention represented a seminal event in the Catholic labor movement, avoiding the establishment of a weakened, European-style US Catholic labor union and the ultimate breach between the church and most US Catholic unionists (Higgins 1993, 49).

Pope Leo XIII's 1891 encyclical on capital and labor, *Rerum Novarum* (*RN*), laid the philosophical groundwork for the church's work with low-wage workers, and remains a timely and powerful touchstone. It responded to the harsh realities of Catholics that had resettled in industrial centers in Europe and the United States in the nineteenth century (McGreevy 2003, 128-129). However, it reads less like an historic artifact and more like a timeless indictment of human greed, self-delusion, and resulting excesses of economic systems that value profit over persons. It makes a powerful case for "justice" in the Catholic sense of establishing "right relationships," giving each person their due, and promoting the common good.

It begins by placing labor challenges in historical context, arguing that the disappearance of guilds and the absence of new "protective organizations" for working people have left working people "surrendered, isolated, and helpless, to the hard-heartedness of employers and the greed of unchecked competition" (*RN* 3).

It makes natural law arguments for private property and for the complementary roles of the "working" and "capital" classes. However, it sharply distinguishes between the right to private ownership and the duty to use private property for the good of all, particularly the indigent (22). It places an affirmative duty on employers to pay "just" wages, to avoid profiting at the expense of poor workers, to refrain from reducing wages through illegitimate means, and to recognize that, "in proportion to their scantiness," the wages of workers should "be accounted sacred" (20).

Rerum Novarum argues that justice "demands" that the working classes share the "benefits which they create" and that the more the state can do "for the benefit of the working classes ... the less need there will be to seek for special means to relieve them" (32, 34). It places on public authorities a special duty to defend the rights of "wage-earners" since the "richer class have many ways of shielding themselves, and stand less in need of help from the State; whereas the poor have no resources of their own to fall back upon, and must chiefly depend upon the assistance of the State" (37). It calls for saving "unfortunate working people from the cruelty of men of greed, who use human beings as mere instruments of money-making" (42). As a practical matter, it calls for "free agreements" between workers and employers, wages sufficient to enable workers to "comfortably" support their families, wider ownership of private property, and labor unions and other associations that benefit workers and "draw the two classes more closely together" (45-49).

In 1919, Father John Ryan, an economist and the long-time director of the US bishops' Social Action Department (SAD), wrote the "Bishops' Program of Social Reconstruction." Ryan's previous scholarship had argued in favor of labor unions, a living wage, and the role of the state in ensuring the dignity of workers (Dolan 1992, 342-343). In the 1919 plan, Ryan proposed

113

sweeping social reforms inspired by Pope Leo XIII's call for "a return to Christian life and Christian institutions" (*RN* 27).

Like *Rerum Novarum*'s prescriptions, many of the proposed reforms were prescient. They included:

- a job program for returning soldiers;
- equal pay for women;
- a "family living wage";
- the right to organize;
- protection against coercion by union members;
- maintenance of wage levels established during the war;
- public housing projects;
- the abolition of monopolistic practices;
- minimum wage laws;
- health, unemployment and old age insurance;
- life insurance for soldiers;
- municipal health clinics for the poor;
- specialized group medical care for workers and their families;
- labor representation in industrial management;
- universal vocational training;
- the abolition of child labor;
- expanded worker ownership of businesses through co-operative societies and co-partnership agreements; and
- regulation of public service monopolies and limitation of their financial returns (National Catholic War Council 1919).

The paper concluded with a call for "reform in the spirit of both labor and capital":

The laborer must come to realize that he owes his employer and society an honest day's work in return for a fair wage, and that conditions cannot be substantially improved until he roots out the desire to get a maximum of return for a minimum of service. The capitalist ... needs to learn the long-forgotten truth that wealth is stewardship, that profit-making is not the basic justification of business enterprise, and that there are such things as fair profits, fair interest and fair prices. (ibid.)

New Deal legislation incorporated all of the proposed recommendations, with the exception of labor participation in management (Baker 2010, 46-47). The Bishops' Program of Social Reconstruction also contributed to the development of the "public religion" or "social Gospel" tradition of the Catholic Church in the United States, laid the groundwork for an ecumenical approach to social justice, and provided the framework for a deeper integration of immigrants into society based on a shared, rights-centered struggle. As Catholic Church historian Jay Dolan describes this evolution, in the nearly three decades between Gibbons' defense of the Knights of Labor and release of the Bishops' Program of Social Construction:

the labor movement had come of age; a progressive reform movement had captured the imagination of Americans; Catholic workers joined unions in large numbers and rose to leadership positions; labor priests began to emerge; and charity workers sought to prevent poverty and social distress .... (Dolan 1992, 345)

For present purposes, the Catholic social tradition arose largely in response to the struggles of immigrants. This tradition was solidified by the release of Pope Pius XI's encyclical *Quadragesimo Anno* (*QA*) on the 40th anniversary of *Rerum Novarum*. Like *Rerum Novarum*, it criticized communism, unfettered capitalism and socialism. However, it distinguished between revolutionary socialism, characterized by "class struggle and the abolition of private ownership," and "more moderate," reform socialism which (it argued) approached "the truths which Christian tradition has always held sacred" and often led to positions that approximated those that "Christian reformers of society justly insist upon" (*QA* 112-113). It also sought cooperation between the government, the labor movement and business. It presented an overarching vision in which "[i]ndustry owners, as good stewards of their properties, would provide for an industry's managers and workers, to share justly in proceeds and production decisions, and the government would pass laws to facilitate such industrial democracy, stepping in only to make certain that this objective was reached" (Baker 2010, 57).

The encyclical praised *Rerum Novarum* as the "Magna Charta upon which all Christian activity in the social field ought to be based" and it affirmed many of its core themes (*QA* 39). For example, it described the "twofold character" of ownership, the right of private ownership, which allows individuals to provide for their families, and the social sense of private property which recognizes that goods are "destined" for the entire human family" and should be used to further the common good (45, 49). It averred that the "immense multitude of the non-owning workers on the one hand and the enormous riches of certain very wealthy men on the other establish an unanswerable argument that the riches which are so abundantly produced in our age of 'industrialism' ... are not rightly distributed and equitably made available to the various classes of people" (60). It argued that workers should be paid sufficient wages to support themselves and their families (71). It also set forth the principal of "subsidiary functions," the idea that "a greater and higher association" should not be assigned to what "lesser and subordinate organizations can do" (79). It endorsed the right to found, adopt and constitute associations with those engaged in the same industry or profession (87). It stressed the dignity of workers and the "social character" of economic activity (101). It argued that even if justice were fully realized, there would still be the need for charity to "bring about [the] union of minds and hearts" that underlies enduring social reform (137).

ii. *Catholic Labor Schools*

One of *Quadragesimo Anno*'s most influential ideas was "side by side" agencies devoted to "imbuing and forming" members of labor unions "in the teaching of religion and morality so that they in turn may be able to permeate the unions with that good spirit which should direct them in their activity" (*QA* 35). This idea inspired the growth of Catholic labor schools, which Monsignor George Higgins called "an early and somewhat raucous form of what we know today as 'adult education'" and which "arose in the context of struggle and confrontation, a time when millions of workers asserted their rights of free association in the workplace" (Higgins 1993, 55).[18]

Dioceses, religious orders, associations and other Catholic institutions sponsored labor schools. Each network and school had its own instructors, strategies, curriculum, sources of support, and relationship with church hierarchy (Baker 2010, 102-103). Classes typically lasted between seven and nine weeks, and covered Catholic social teaching, parliamentary procedure, public speaking, basic economics, labor law and history, logic,

---

18 Monsignor George Higgins served as assistant director of the US bishop's Social Action Department from 1944 to 1954 and its director from 1954 to 1980. For most of the twentieth century, he was an active and often leading participant in the Catholic Church's engagement on labor issues. In 2000, he was awarded the Presidential Medal of Freedom. Higgins has been credited with extending the church's already legendary work with laborers to the struggles of migrant laborers. Higgins met César Chávez, co-founder of the United Farm Workers (UFW) and a devout Catholic, at a social action meeting at Boston College (Baker 2010, 248-249). He also worked to extend labor rights globally, including through support of the Polish solidarity movement.

labor ethics, and organizing (ibid., 20-21, 197). While providing technical knowledge that allowed participants to advance within their unions, the schools also had a broader mission; i.e., to teach workers to view their jobs as religious vocations and to reshape industrial society and the workplace in terms of Catholic values (McShane 1990, 291-292). Labor priests argued that unions countered the conditions that gave rise to communism and fascism, and represented a "middle-of-the-road" solution to address the "'unbearable wrongs'" suffered in the workplace (ibid.,199).

In 1937, a group of Catholic unionists founded the Association of Catholic Trade Unionists (ACTU) in New York (Morris 1997, 211-212; Baker 2010, 60). Its founders viewed ACTU as the kind of "side by side" entity urged by Pope Pius XI in *Quadragesimo Anno*. By 1940, it had spread to fifteen cities. ACTU sponsored labor schools, published a newspaper, and actively supported more than 300 strikes between 1939 and 1949 (Dolan 1992, 405). Members, who called themselves "Actists," fought organized crime on New York's waterfront and communist infiltration of the United Electrical Workers (Morris 1997, 209). They were particularly active in the struggles of the Congress of Industrial Organizations and the United Auto Workers in the 1940s. During this period, Catholics comprised more than one-half of union members (210).

A SAD survey in 1939 showed that 52 schools operated in 24 cities (42-43). By the 1940s, this ministry had spread to encompass more than 150 schools (20). In 1938, SAD sponsored its first National Catholic Social Action conference, which drew 1,000 students, 750 priests, 25 bishops, and speakers representing labor, management, and organizers (typically priests) in particular industries (33). At the time, SAD sponsored nine Schools of Social Action to train priests and lay people on labor issues (35). During the SAD proceedings in 1938, Father John Hayes, a labor activist, described the vision of the church in organizing as follows:

> The meat-packing business or any business is meant to be part of an integrated system, a universe divinely ordained to provide for the material as well as the spiritual needs of every human. Business has tried to secede from that whole; we have tried to subtract part of God's creation—the economic part—from God's dominion. (34)

In 1940, the Society of Jesus founded its Institute for Social Order (ISO) which coordinated Jesuit labor schools, including the Xavier Labor School (XLS) in lower Manhattan and other social action initiatives (Baker 2010, 229-30; Morris 1997, 215; McShane 1990, 289, 291). By 1943, 375 students attended XLS each year (Baker 2010, 219). John Sweeney, future President of the AFL-CIO, attended the school in 1955 (113). Its long-time director, Father Phillip Carey, S.J. wrote that "the concept of solidarity of all workers is nothing but a weak version of the Communion of Saints and the participation of all of us in the Mystical Body of Christ" (233).

The Brooklyn Priests' Social Action Committee sponsored 23 schools (with 2,000 students) in the 1950s, including in parishes, high schools, and Knights of Columbus halls. Three "institutes" offered advanced courses for students that had taken its basic course of study (105-106). This network followed a typical trajectory, shrinking to just two schools by 1960 (113).

The decline in labor schools and priests in the late 1950s has been attributed to multiple factors, including:

- passage of the Taft-Hartley Act in 1948, which allowed states to outlaw union shops and paved the way for "right to work" legislation;

119

- the growing economic clout and success of American Catholics, which diminished their need for unions;
- a shortage of priests and a generation of priests less interested in labor issues;
- the overall decline of labor union membership;
- the challenges presented to unions by globalization; and
- the illiteracy of Catholics in the natural law tradition.

The virtual disappearance of labor schools does not imply that Catholic institutions and leaders have not remained engaged with low-wage laborers, particularly immigrants. "Labor priests" have never gone away, though many priests and other vowed religious who work extensively on worker justice issues no longer characterize their work in this way. In researching a report on low-wage immigrant laborers, the Catholic Legal Immigration Network, Inc. relied heavily on priests and vowed religious who minister to day laborers, farmworkers, meat-packing and poultry processing workers (CLINIC 2000).

Catholic institutions have established and actively supported "worker centers" which offer immigrants job placement, employer screening, legal assistance, English language classes, training on labor and immigration law, and other services (Fine 2005, 1-2). St. Pius V Parish in Chicago's Lower West Side, for example, helped to start a day labor coalition that formed the Chicago Workers' Collaborative in the Pilsen neighborhood. The parish served as the fiscal sponsor of this organization and Father Brendan Curran, the pastor of St. Pius V, remains the group's secretary. The parish, he says, is "the place where people find shelter in the midst of immigration coming down hard on certain industries/ businesses on the one hand, and the underbelly of places that don't operate with any rules on the other." He credits the Chicago Workers' Collaborative with helping to pass an amendment to the Illinois Wage Payment and Collection Act, which substantially strengthened the state's wage theft provisions.

The Catholic Migrant Farmworker Network provides pastoral support to migrant farmers, inviting them to participate in parish life and often accompanying them on their seasonal journeys. It also serves as a liaison between farmworkers and the legal, social and advocacy organizations that assist them.

The US bishops also regularly meet with the leaders of labor unions, visit worker camps, and support collective bargaining. The bishops devoted their annual Labor Day Statement in 2006 to immigrant laborers and the theme of building community based on shared values:

> Immigrants come seeking to provide a decent living for their families, dreaming of a better life for their children, hoping to make a contribution. These are the deeply held American values we celebrate on Labor Day. The principles of our faith and the traditions of our nation call us to welcome those who share these values and hopes. They add vitality and energy, diversity and hope to our communities and our country. Together, we can build a better nation, a stronger economy and a more faithful Church. (USCCB 2006)

Catholic leaders have also played an active role in inter-faith initiatives for workplace justice, including through the Chicago-based Inter-faith Committee for Worker Justice.

iii. *Need for Greater Engagement with Business and Labor*

Several factors argue in favor of greater Catholic engagement with immigrant laborers. Union membership has plummeted from 39 percent of the US workforce in 1954 to 11.3 percent today and just 6.6 percent of the private sector workforce. Inequality has increased, and the social safety net has diminished. There are significant gaps in core US labor and workplace protection laws, insufficient enforcement of existing laws, and rampant violations in certain industries and occupations with high concentrations of low-wage immigrant workers (Kerwin 2013b, 43-45). In addition, a historically large, heavily Catholic, unauthorized population, coupled with unprecedented immigration enforcement activities, increases the need for strong mediating agencies and safe settings where immigrants can build community and become "visible" as human beings (Odem 2004, 42).

Maria Elena Durazo, a parishioner at Dolores Mission Church in Los Angeles, is the former executive secretary and treasurer of the Los Angeles County Federation of Labor for the American Federation of Labor and Congress of Industrial Organizations (AFL-CIO). She has also chaired the AFL-CIO's national immigration committee. Durazo sees the potential for a more significant institutional commitment by Catholic institutions to low-wage immigrant laborers.

According to Durazo, the labor movement, the Archdiocese of Los Angeles, and immigrant rights advocates became "strategic partners" in Los Angeles in the mid- to late 1990s. She credits Cardinal Roger Mahony for serving as "a public spokesperson for low-wage immigrant workers." The archdiocese supported the Janitors for Justice movement, revived the tradition of the Labor Day mass, supported the 2003 immigrant workers' Freedom Ride, pushed for immigration reform post-9/11, and initiated a mass to honor César Chávez.[19] Labor unions also work with

---

19   Many of Chávez's well-known sayings bear the stamp of his faith, whether on
      person-centered economic arrangements ("The fight is never about grapes or
      lettuce. It is always about people"); culture ("Preservation of one's own culture

parishes on local immigrant rights issues, including immigration enforcement and policing tactics that marginalize and endanger immigrants. Durazo argues that unions "bring to the table political relationships that aren't necessarily there for the parishes." Parishes, in turn, represent a source of "rank and file members, people who vote and make a difference."

Durazo also draws a connection between social justice, labor organizing and immigrant integration, and sees legalization and citizenship services as an area of potential collaboration:

> When 28 percent of Los Angeles earns poverty wages while working full time, that should be of concern to everyone. This has to be addressed in a more organized way. That is part of immigrant integration to this country. Individual unions take up different aspects of integration for their particular membership; but there is not a coordinated network of services along those lines. Many unions do citizenship; others do nonpartisan civic participation, such as get out the vote. With the [legalization] reform proposal, it is overwhelming to think about how we would address those needs.

Durazo lauds the work of Clergy and Laity United for Economic Justice (CLUE), a national, inter-denominational organization that promotes workers' rights in the context of religious beliefs and values. CLUE was particularly active in supporting the hotel workers' living wage campaign in California in 2012. However, she hopes that the Catholic Church will take "head-on" the issue of "workers and their wellbeing in the workplace." She sees a strong convergence of values and interests, and immense potential benefits from a greater relationship between the church and labor unions on these issues:

---

does not require contempt or disrespect of other cultures"); or community ("You are never strong enough that you don't need help").

The church, as well as the labor movement, has an extraordinary infrastructure that nobody else has ... We're the only two institutions that have the trust, the reach, the experience, the history, and the potential for the volunteers as part of the resources. We each have to decide we're going to do something dramatically different than what we have ever done before. By joining together, we really are more than one plus one. The church wants to be seen as opening the doors to immigrants. Well, so does labor. We want to be seen as the future of these workers, that's what we try to do every day.

One of the most promising Catholic integration developments has been the recent formation of a new network of labor priests. The Reverend Cletus Kiley, the immigration policy director for UNITE-HERE,[20] was instrumental in constituting a group of 28 priests in Chicago from May 21-25, 2012.[21] Kiley believes that immigrant laborers—in an era of globalization, significant workplace abuses, and lack of regulation—need labor unions, and immigrants, in turn, present an opportunity to strengthen the Catholic Church's connection to labor. Prior to inviting priests to participate, the Labor Priests Initiative sought permission from their bishops. Most of the priests had been ordained for ten years or less.

---

20 UNITE HERE represents workers throughout the United States and Canada who work in the hotel, gaming, food service, manufacturing, textile, distribution, laundry, and airport industries.

21 The network enjoys broad institutional support. It has been developed in close consultation with the National Federation of Priest Councils, the US Conference of Catholic Bishops, the Council of Major Superiors of Men, the Catholic Labor Network, Catholic Scholars for Worker Justice, the Kalmanovitz Center for Labor and the Working Poor at Georgetown University, the AFL-CIO's Executive Council, Pax Romana, Interfaith Worker Justice, the Merton Institute, and the Monsignor Egan Office of Urban Education and Community Partnerships at DePaul University. It has convened under the auspices of several of these entities.

As in the past, this fledgling community has been inspired by immigrant workers and Catholic social teaching. Pope Benedict XVI's 2009 encyclical *Caritas in Veritate* (*CV*), has been a particular touchstone of the group, as has a 2012 reflection on the "Vocation of the Business Leader" (VB) by the Pontifical Council for Justice and Peace.

Caritas in Veritate views labor from the lens of human development and globalization. It decries the "downsizing of social security systems" which result from competition between states seeking to attract foreign business, and "the consequent grave danger for the rights of workers, for fundamental human rights and for solidarity associated with the traditional forms of the social State" (*CV* 25). It urges business to assume responsibility for the well-being, not just of investors, but for "all stakeholders who contribute to the life of the business," including workers (40). It describes migration as "a social phenomenon of epoch-making proportions," recognizes the contributions of immigrant workers to the economic development of host countries, and argues that they should not be treated as a "commodity" or "factor of production" (62). It affirms the church's commitment to a global coalition in support of "decent work," defined as:

> work that expresses the essential dignity of every man and woman in the context of their particular society: work that is freely chosen, effectively associating workers, both men and women, with the development of their community; work that enables the worker to be respected and free from any form of discrimination; work that makes it possible for families to meet their needs and provide schooling for their children, without the children themselves being forced into labor; work that permits the workers to organize themselves freely, and to make their voices heard; work that leaves enough room for rediscovering one's roots at a personal, familial and spiritual level; work that guarantees those who have retired a decent standard of living. (63)

125

DONALD KERWIN, WITH BREANA GEORGE

It also strongly endorses labor unions and urges them to "turn their attention" to workers in developing countries (64).

Building on *Caritas in Veritate*, the "Vocation of the Business Leader" provides an important reference point for the emerging network of "labor priests," who have prioritized engagement of Catholic business leaders. The document seeks a commercial system that serves the "common good"; e.g., one in which "customers receive goods and services at fair prices; employees engage in good work and earn a livelihood for themselves and their families; and investors earn a reasonable return on their investment" (VB 2). It urges business people not to divide "the demands" of faith from work (10). It argues that the context of business has substantially changed over the last quarter century due to globalization, ease of communication, the economic shift from production to finance, and "individualism," tied to moral relativism (17).

It calls on business leaders to honor human dignity and serve the common good by:

- "creating goods which are truly good and services which truly serve";
- demonstrating solidarity with the poor (serving "deprived and underserved" populations);
- fostering dignified work;
- promoting subsidiarity by giving employees a voice and say in their work;
- serving as good stewards of capital, human and environmental resources; and,
- fairly allocating resources to all of the stakeholders in the business (40-56).

At the May 2012 training, each priest committed to report back to his bishop and presbyteral council (council of priests),

126

and to speak to at least two other priests in depth about the ministry, as well as to a local labor leader. By October 2014, the Labor Priest Initiative had expanded to include 170 priests, and had been situated in the National Federation of Priests' Council. The US Association of Catholic Priests, an organization of roughly 1,000 priests (many retired), has also formed a labor caucus and is working to mentor younger priests. The Labor Priest Initiative has held meetings in several dioceses with priests, bishops and local labor leaders to review the local situation of working people, with a special eye on the plight of immigrant workers. In doing so, it seeks to make the network of labor priests a concrete, local reality. The success of this ministry—as part of a larger, more extensive engagement with business leaders, employers and immigrant workers—should be an institutional priority for the Catholic Church in the years ahead.

6. IMMIGRANT SERVICE AND CHARITABLE NETWORKS

The US bishops' Migration and Refugee Services division, CLINIC, its national legal agency for immigrants, and Catholic Charities USA (CCUSA) support overlapping networks of local Catholic agencies and programs that directly serve and advocate for immigrants. Collectively, these agencies and their predecessors represent nearly a century of sustained commitment to immigrants by the Catholic Church in the United States.

i. *Migration and Refugee Services*

In December 1920, the US bishops created a Bureau of Immigration to respond to the continued influx of European immigrants. The Bureau established offices in major port cities on the East Coast, including New York City, Boston and Philadelphia.

It also opened a border office in El Paso, Texas to support migrants from Mexico. These offices met incoming migrants at ports-of-entry, offering them legal aid, resettlement, and other assistance.

With the onset of World War II, the National Catholic Welfare Conference (NCWC) began to focus on the millions of displaced persons who lived in camps across Europe. NCWC established the National Catholic Resettlement Council (NCRC) in 1947 to advocate for legislation to assist them. Following passage of the Displaced Persons Act in 1948, NCWC helped incoming Catholics to clear customs, reunite with family, and make transportation connections to their destinations. Between 1945 and 1956, it assisted 800,000 persons. The Bureau of Immigration became the United States Catholic Conference's Migration and Refugee Services' division in 1965.

MRS coordinates the US bishops' immigration policy and advocacy work, including the national Justice for Immigrants campaign for federal immigration reform. Its network directly serves refugees, asylees, minors not accompanied by their parents or guardians, and survivors of human trafficking. Since 1975, MRS has resettled more than one million refugees. To put this figure in context, MRS has resettled more refugees over the last 37 years than any *nation* in the world, with the exception of the United States. Through partnerships with nearly 100 Catholic Charities or dioceses across the country and through contracts with the federal government, MRS receives, places and orients refugees in their new communities and provides them with intensive, coordinated case management services aimed at self-sufficiency through employment. It provides employment-readiness services to eligible refugees, asylees, Cuban and Haitian entrants, and survivors of human trafficking. In the past fifteen years, MRS has also served over 180,000 Cuban and

Haitian entrants, who are eligible to receive the same services and benefits as refugees.

The US refugee program does not track long-term integration outcomes. Nor does it limit admission to refugees who can be employed or integrated. To the contrary, MRS prides itself on resettling the most vulnerable cases, including people with difficult medical conditions and single mothers. It provides "integrated" services in collaboration with Catholic Charities, dioceses, parishes, government entities, employers, and non-Catholic charitable institutions. As a result, even with difficult case loads, MRS has historically achieved higher than average rates of self-sufficiency outcomes in its Match Grant Program.[22] It is expected that roughly 70 percent of those enrolled in the program will become self-sufficient through employment within 180 days of their arrival to the United States. In recent years, the MRS network has had a 50 percent self-sufficiency rate at 120 days and, of those cases, 90 percent remain self-sufficient 180 days after arrival.

Given the short window of government-supported resettlement services, it is particularly important that refugees be located within supportive communities. In 2010, MRS created the Parishes Organized to Welcome Refugees (POWR) program to support parish-based work with refugees. The program recruits volunteers, forms community partnerships, and connects newly arrived refugees with volunteers who provide mentoring, social

---

22   Administered by the US Department of Health and Human Services (DHHS), the Match Grant program assists refugees in achieving economic self-sufficiency within 120-180 days after arrival. Voluntary agencies "match" funding from the Office of Refugee Resettlement (ORR) with cash and contributions of goods and services. The program enhances the assistance given to refugees through the US Department of State's Reception and Placement program which provides support for integration within the refugee's first 90 days after arrival.

connections, language and job skills and other integration services that go beyond federal programs. In its first four years, the program recruited 10,000 volunteers and raised $10 million in cash and in-kind donations.

MRS is one of two US agencies that resettle unaccompanied refugee children. The Unaccompanied Refugee Minors (URM) program provides foster care services to unaccompanied foreign-born children living in the United States, including child victims of trafficking, children with asylum status, Cuban and Haitian entrant children and children with Special Immigrant Juvenile Status. In addition to placing children in foster care, MRS specializes in the reunification of children who have been separated from their families. Through a network of over 100 local service providers, MRS assesses unaccompanied, unauthorized children who have been apprehended by immigration officials to determine appropriate placement and family reunification alternatives to detention and it provides case management and family support assistance. It has led the church's multi-faceted response to the immense increase in 2014 in migration to the United States of unaccompanied children (68,541 arrested along the US-Mexico border) and parents with children (68,445 arrested), particularly from the Northern Triangle nations of Central America (DHS-CBP 2014).

MRS' long history of work with the most vulnerable has afforded it substantial expertise in the area of human trafficking. Its recent anti-trafficking initiatives include a national education campaign, the Amistad Movement, and the Dignity of Work Program, which provides enhanced employment services to survivors who are not eligible to be enrolled in traditional employment programs. While the goal of the Amistad Movement is prevention and education, mainly in immigrant communities, the goal of Dignity of Work is to reach those most marginalized in their journeys of reintegration and restoration. MRS convenes the Coalition of Catholic Organizations against Human Trafficking (CCOAHT), which is comprised of religious communities, Catholic universities and other Catholic organizations that seek to educate Catholics about church teaching on human trafficking and to build collaborations and initiatives in this area.

ii. *Catholic Legal Immigration Network, Inc.*

CLINIC was founded in 1988 in response to the US bishops' recognition of the increasing need for legal services by the nation's record immigrant population. The US bishops had historically run legal immigration programs in four dioceses. In 1993, they made a strategic decision to turn CLINIC into a legal support agency, with the goal of expanding, training, and supporting diocesan legal service programs. The Catholic principle of subsidiarity has since guided CLINIC's programmatic commitments: it seeks to empower and support local immigration programs and initiatives, while taking on work that dioceses cannot easily assume themselves.

Over the last 20 years, CLINIC's network has expanded from 17 legal programs to more than 260 programs which serve hundreds of thousands of immigrants each year in more than 400 locations and 46 states, the District of Columbia and Puerto Rico. Most of these offices operate within diocesan Catholic Charities agencies. Thus, CLINIC's work might be viewed as a model for how to expand the scope of an established network of Catholic institutions, the nation's largest charitable social service network, in response to the needs of immigrants.

CLINIC's network receives only minimal government funding. Its expansion attests to the demand for legal and related

131

services and to the commitment of the mostly immigrant, "accredited" non-attorneys who staff its affiliated programs. CLINIC also administers multi-site programs that operate through local agencies, including citizenship, ESL classes, and immigrant-led community organizing initiatives. It carries out the latter in partnership with CCHD. Immigrant integration is the explicit goal of these programs. CLINIC's web-site features successful integration programs developed by its local affiliates.

CLINIC also leads a nation-wide planning process to implement a large-scale legalization program, whether resulting from federal legislation or Executive action. It views legalization as a potentially unifying Catholic institutional priority. In addition, the CLINIC network's expertise and experience in serving low-income and vulnerable populations informs the agency's administrative advocacy (before federal agencies) and the US bishops' public policy work before Congress and the Executive branch.

iii. *Catholic Charities USA*

The National Conference of Catholic Charities (NCCC) was founded in 1910 to inventory and professionalize Catholic charitable work, promote diocesan Catholic Charities agencies, create solidarity among the church's charitable entities, and serve as "an attorney for the poor" (Brown and McKeown 1997, 62-63). In 1986, NCCC became Catholic Charities USA (CCUSA).

CCUSA operates as the trade association for diocesan Catholic Charities agencies. In 2013, 151 of its member agencies (86 percent of respondents) reported providing 17.3 million services to more than 9 million "unduplicated" clients (CCUSA 2014, 2-3). Catholic Charities agencies offer food, social support, education, enrichment, family-strengthening, housing, disaster relief, and other services. They also partner extensively with parishes. In 2013, these agencies provided legal and other immigration-related services to 375,000 persons. In addition, 64 agencies reported helping 21,446 refugees to achieve self-sufficiency (15-16). Catholic Charities also offer significant integration services (like English and civics classes), and services to vulnerable immigrant populations, including survivors of human trafficking and domestic abuse.

In 2005, the Catholic Charities network made immigration its national policy priority, the first time it had adopted a network-wide priority of this kind. Its statement on immigration, which was unanimously approved at the Catholic Charities USA annual meeting, asserted that the needs of newcomers "go well beyond immigration status" and include "work, education, health care, civic participation and homeownership" (CCUSA 2005, 21). The statement criticized the lack of a coordinated national program "to respond to immigrants' multi-faceted integration needs" (ibid.). It ended with a call to "solidarity" and a commitment to building the necessary "structures" of solidarity:

> [W]e commit to acting in greater solidarity with migrants and newcomers. We vow to help educate Catholics on the Church's social teaching, its migrant heritage and its work with newcomers. We pledge to be more active advocates for our newly arrived brothers and sisters. We vow to evaluate our commitments and to measure our work based on our concrete experience of the needs and aspirations of newcomers. We commit to reorienting our agencies and, if necessary, to creating new institutions to serve the needs of newcomers more fully. We pledge to support and collaborate more significantly with institutions—like immigrant-led organizing agencies and labor unions—that seek to empower immigrants. We hope to serve today's newcomers as devotedly as the Church served our parents, grandparents and other ancestors. (26)

Catholic Charities agencies typically serve as the focal point for diocesan legal immigration, refugee resettlement, and integration services more broadly. These agencies offer inter-connected services that seek to promote justice, meet material and spiritual needs, and empower individuals, families and communities. As Sister RayMonda Duvall, the director of Catholic Charities of the Diocese of San Diego puts it, "we provide integrated services, which allow us to help integrate immigrants." Catholic Charities of the Diocese of San Diego also "integrates" its work with other Catholic and non-Catholic partner institutions with the goal of promoting integral development. Among its other programs, the agency runs a large and creative refugee resettlement program, a legal services program, family support services, and a shelter for immigrant women and children. In 2013, it opened a shelter for migrant workers that had been in development for four years.

iv. Parish-based Charities: Casa San Bernardo (Riverdale, Maryland)[23]

While not as visible as diocesan charitable agencies, parishes provide significant direct services to immigrants and have been a locus of community organizing. The combined parish of St. Bernard of Clairvaux and Our Lady of Fatima in Riverdale Park, Maryland in suburban Washington, DC is an "intercultural"

---

23   Casa San Juan in Tucson, Arizona is another exemplary parish-based charity. In 2002, St. John the Evangelist Catholic Church opened Casa San Juan as an immigrant welcoming center. The center, which serves roughly 200 persons per week, emerged from a collaboration between the Diocese of Tucson, Pima County Interfaith Council and parish leaders. It assists the poor, including migrants, through a community food bank, and refers immigrants to direct service organizations. In addition, the Arizona Attorney General has located a satellite office at the center which provides information and assistance on consumer fraud and rights violations. The center also offers a monthly mobile health clinic with the University of Arizona.

parish, one in which diverse parishioners "are not in isolated tracks or silos, but more or less continuously rub shoulders" (Deck 2013, 43). Its seven person pastoral team consists entirely of immigrants. Roughly 90 percent of its parishioners come from Mexico, Central America, Asia, Africa, Europe, and other regions of the world.

St. Bernard was established in 1948 and Our Lady of Fatima in 1999. In 2005, following a fire, Our Lady of Fatima began to use the facilities of St. Bernard for religious and social services. St. Bernard is a predominantly Latino(a) parish, while Our Lady of Fatima primarily serves Portuguese, Brazilians and Cape Verdeans.

Affordable housing in the area attracts a continual stream of immigrants who typically stay long enough to become established in the United States before settling elsewhere. Father Sérgio Dall'Agnese, a member of the Scalabrinian congregation which was founded in Italy in the late nineteenth century to serve migrants, is its pastor. When he asks each week who among the congregation is a recent arrival, multiple people raise their hands.

The parish holds masses and religious education programs in English, Portuguese and Spanish. Its parish council consists of parishioners from all of the church's immigrant and linguistic groups. Its members come together for trilingual liturgies, Thanksgiving Mass, Holy Week, Christmas and confirmation. Parishioners bring flags of their countries of origin to Thanksgiving Mass. Father Sérgio views pastoral events as an opportunity to share culture and values in a religious space, which helps to ease tensions across immigrant groups and within the Spanish-speaking community. On the issue of integration, he explains:

> The main message is that we are Catholics, one church, one faith, and we are brothers and sisters. There is no push to become

135

American; it is a process. You keep your culture, and accept a new culture.

Families attend mass together and, therefore, church for US-born children is in their parents' native language. The parish has found that immigrant parents want religious education for their children to be in Spanish or Portuguese so that their household connection with faith and prayer is not lost.

According to Father Sérgio, immigrants from rural communities in Latin America are accustomed to turning to a parish for all forms of support. In the United States, their reliance upon and trust in the church is reinforced by fear of approaching other institutions and lack of information on how to address their needs. A primary reason why people come to St. Bernard is to seek assistance in securing food, a place to sleep, counseling and crisis support.

In 2009, the parish established a nonprofit organization Casa San Bernardo, Inc. to house the growing social component of its ministry to immigrants. The agency's mission is "to educate individuals and families to become contributors and promoters of a new society by strengthening the values of respect and self-determination."

Casa San Bernardo is staffed by a volunteer team led by two religious sisters. It provides counseling; translation and interpretation services; assistance with filling out forms for school, government, medical or employment purposes; preventative health screenings; and information and referrals to social service agencies. It also offers educational programs including ESL, computer literacy classes, and citizenship preparation. Of all its services, the greatest demand is for English instruction, especially from the mothers of young children.

To support immigrant parents, Casa San Bernardo runs an unofficial pre-school program that promotes school readiness. In conjunction with learning English, mothers learn basic computer literacy with the goal of being able to access teacher messages and to read report cards from their children's schools. The organization has sought to include all members of the parish in the process of immigrant education. Often, this starts with a push for newcomers to register with the parish. The parish secretary explains to families that while not a practice in their home countries, registering is a first step to establishing a record of their presence in the United States that may be ultimately important for addressing their immigration status. Father Sérgio provides letters of support for parishioner applications for immigration benefits, including through the DACA program.

Casa San Bernardo also strengthens the parish's partnerships with other entities. The Mexican Consulate maintains a strong outreach presence at the church to assist people with passports and other paperwork on site. The parish invites police officers to give presentations to parents and teens about gang and drug prevention, and encourages immigrants to interface with police about community affairs. Casa San Bernardo works with the Catholic Charities' Parish Partners program to refer people to services that the parish is not able to provide directly, including legal services. In short, Casa San Bernardo both integrates church services and acts as an integrating institution for its parishioners within the broader community.

7. CATHOLIC HEALTH CARE ORGANIZATIONS

The origins of Catholic health care in the United States can be traced to small groups of religious sisters who responded to requests from religious and secular leaders to serve the poor in particular communities.[24] Their work predates the establishment of the nation. In August 1727, a small group of French Ursuline nuns, a novice, and two others arrived in New Orleans and opened the first women's convent in the United States (Fanning 1908). The Ursulines, teaching sisters, established a school and orphanage, but also nursed the sick (Farren 1996, iii-iv). This set the pattern for the next two hundred years, as religious orders of sisters arrived in communities and met whatever needs they found among the people, even needs beyond the scope of their traditional ministries.

Catholic sisters staffed public and private hospitals and established their own hospitals (Kauffman 1995; Farren 1996), primarily in cities with "high concentrations of poor immigrants" (White 2000, 17). Sisters from 21 religious communities served as nurses for Union and Confederate soldiers during the Civil War (Kauffman 1995, 83). In the late nineteenth and early twentieth centuries, sisters distinguished themselves during outbreaks of cholera, small pox, and typhoid (Farren 1996, 20-29). Many died tending to those who would otherwise have been abandoned.

The Catholic Health Association of the United States (CHA) includes more than 2,000 Catholic health care systems, hospitals, long-term care facilities, and related entities. Catholic health care organizations—hospitals, clinics, hospices, and other facilities—seek to maintain their commitment to the poor and vulnerable, while attending to "the whole person," in an increasingly profit-driven field (CHA 2013). They serve a disproportionate share of low-income Medicare, Medicaid and uninsured patients.[25]

---

24   The calls came from bishops, pastors, mayors, local doctors and philanthropists.
25   Letter from Carol Keehan, President and CEO of The Catholic Health Association, to Senator Max Baucus and Senator Charles Grassley, 27 May 2009. http://www.chausa.org/docs/default-source/advocacy/dbd926dc9d574f5abcc9fdd42-f475f9d1-pdf.pdf?sfvrsn=2

i. *Community Benefit Programs*

Catholic hospitals have been particular leaders in community benefit programs, which seek to improve access to healthcare; enhance community health; advance medical or health knowledge; and relieve or reduce the health improvement burden on government. The IRS has adopted a "community benefit standard" as the basis for tax-exempt status. Programs range from health education to financial assistance for the unreimbursed costs of serving patients enrolled in Medicaid and the Children's Insurance Programs. Under the Patient Protection and Affordable Care Act of 2010, tax-exempt hospitals must conduct a Community Health Needs Assessment at least every three years and develop implementation strategies to meet the needs identified in the assessments.

CHA has developed uniform standards for nonprofit hospitals in community benefit planning and reporting. In assessing community needs, hospitals look to indicators that contribute to health disparities like limited English proficiency, low-education levels, subsistence at below the federal poverty line, unemployment, and lack of health insurance. Catholic hospitals do not request information on immigration status, but they provide significant service to unauthorized immigrants, victims of human trafficking, refugees, and others who meet these criteria.

Catholic hospitals meet the needs of immigrant populations within the framework of their service to low-income, uninsured and vulnerable populations. Most hospitals do not formally articulate service to immigrants within their community benefit implementation strategies, but many target immigrant communities and partner with immigrant-based community organizations in carrying out programs and activities. The 16 hospitals in the St. Joseph Health system, for example, contribute 10 percent of their net income to a community partnership fund, which makes grants to community organizations that serve the vulnerable, including immigrants without legal status (Robles et al. 2014).

ii. *Specific Initiatives with Immigrants*

Catholic health programs are also taking a targeted approach to providing care to immigrants. In Portland, Oregon, for example, the community health division of Providence Health and Services has partnered with Catholic Charities and the University of Portland to implement a health ministry in 14 parishes that serves 7,000 people annually. The Parish Health Promoters/ *Promotores de Salud*[26] program trains volunteer lay leaders to serve as liaisons between the Latino(a) immigrant community, churches and healthcare providers. The *promotores* participate in a 15-week training delivered in Spanish which equips them to provide referrals to health-related services, presentations on health topics, interpretation for medical appointments, information on accessing financial assistance, hospital tours for Spanish-speaking patients, blood pressure checks after mass, and help with completing medical paperwork. According to

---

26   The Department of Health and Human Services Office of Minority Health defines *Promotores de Salud*/Community Health Workers (CHWs) as "volunteer community members who...generally share the ethnicity, language, socioeconomic status, and life experiences of the community they serve. These social attributes and trusting relationships enable [them] to serve as a liaison, link, or intermediary between health and social services and the community to facilitate access to and enrollment in services and improve the quality and cultural competence of service... Additionally *Promotores*/CHWs build individual and community capacity by increasing health knowledge and self-sufficiency through a range of activities such as outreach, community education, informal counseling, social support, and advocacy among communities such as Hispanic/Latino(a) communities." Retrieved from http://minorityhealth.hhs. gov/templates/content.aspx?lvl=2&lvlid=207&ID=8930.

Catholic Charities, the *promotores* "provide a valuable feedback loop to the health system in terms of cultural competency and services to the poor and vulnerable."[27] University students also facilitate preventive dental care clinics at churches, providing low-cost oral exams, dental cleanings and fluoride treatments. According to Providence Health and Services, dental needs are one of the most common reasons that immigrants visit hospital emergency rooms.

Immigrants also work at high rates in health care occupations that lack sufficient US workers (Ewing 2009, 2). Foreign medical graduates, for example, play an oversized role in meeting primary care needs in medically underserved areas and health professional shortage areas (Crawford 2014).

Catholic health care programs have also prioritized providing employment opportunities to newcomers. In Anchorage, the Providence Alaska Medical Center has partnered with Catholic Social Services' Refugee Assistance and Immigration Services, the only state-sponsored resettlement program in Alaska, to help refugees obtain self-sufficiency through employment. The refugee population comes from diverse countries, including Thailand, Laos, Burma, Bhutan, Iran, Iraq, Yemen, Russia, Ukraine, Uzbekistan, Sudan, Somalia, Togo, the Democratic Republic of the Congo (former Zaire), Gambia and Cuba. To respond to the employment needs of refugees with limited English language proficiency, Providence Alaska Medical Center has created special paid trainee positions for environmental and laundry assistants. Through these positions, refugees develop marketable language and other employment skills in a supportive environment with one of Alaska's largest private employers.

---

27   *Parish Health Promoter Program.* Retrieved from http://www.catholiccharities-oregon.org/promotores.asp.

In Iowa, Mercy College of Health Services, the Iowa Bureau of Refugee Services and the Iowa Department of Workforce Development have collaborated on an initiative that offers health sciences education, tutoring, job placement services, and support for refugees. This program provides a pathway to health care positions like emergency medical technician, nursing assistant, medication aid, medical assistant, paramedic and surgical technologist. The program also facilitates health services to immigrants by training staff who can serve the growing non-English speaking population in Iowa. Employer partners include Mercy Health Network, Dallas County Hospital, Buena Vista Regional Medical Center, Bishop Drumm Retirement Center and Arbor Springs. The Mercy Health Network is part of Catholic Health Initiatives, the third largest Catholic health system in the United States. Mercy College is the only higher education entity within this network. To date, the program has granted certification to 159 students from 30 different countries.

Like other Catholic ministries, health care providers have found that "integrated" services allow them to provide their core services more effectively. In Newport News, Virginia, the Bon Secours Mary Immaculate Hospital's Family Focus program offers ESL classes for adults (with child care) and parent/child education classes to promote good parenting practices (Stovsky 2014). These programs allow parents to communicate with doctor's offices, take a more active role in their children's education, and improve their parenting practices. They have also reduced isolation among immigrant parents.

IV. Catholic Institutions and Immigrants: the Convergence of Faith, Needs and Gifts

1. Integration Needs and Priorities

Immigrant integration is typically measured over generations. According to classic assimilation theory, immigrant groups steadily advance in education and occupation and ultimately converge with majority groups in terms of "norms, values, behaviors, and characteristics" (Brown and Bean 2006). Under this theory, each succeeding generation becomes more a part of the mainstream and less distinct in language, residence, and marriage patterns.

Over the last 20 years, classic assimilation theory has been supplanted by segmented assimilation theory, which emphasizes that diverse populations integrate on different timelines and can move in different socio-economic and cultural directions, including into "oppositional" sectors of society. The theory highlights "modes of incorporation" that influence integration outcomes, including government policies that apply to different groups; the values, prejudices and reception of receiving societies; and the characteristics, including the moral and material resources, of co-ethnic communities (Portes and Zhou 1993, 83).[1]

---

1   This theory assumes the lack of a uniformly accessible "mainstream."

The reception of the first generation establishes "the conditions" for the assimilation of the second generation (Haller, Portes and Lynch 2011, 734). This can lead to a "paradox": first-generation immigrants who are poorer and less educated than their progeny, but also healthier, less likely to head single-parent households, and less likely to commit crimes (Matovina 2012, 225). Racial prejudice, settlement in inner-city communities and diminished paths to upward mobility in the post-industrial economy particularly affect the second and third generations.

A study of second-generation youth from 77 nationalities in Miami-Ft. Lauderdale, Florida and San Diego, California illustrates divergent integration outcomes by nation of ancestry. The study included an initial survey of 5,262 eighth and ninth graders in the early 1990s, followed by interviews with 4,288 of the original respondents three years later, and a second follow-up interview with 3,613 of the respondents 10 years after the original survey. The percent of respondents that dropped out of high school or did not continue their education after high school ranged from 6.8 percent of persons of Chinese and Korean descent, to 25.7 percent of Nicaraguans, 37.9 percent of Mexican Americans in California, and 47 percent of Cambodian and Laotian refugees (Haller, Portes, and Lynch 2011, 741). More than 18 percent of second generation West Indian youth and 17 percent of Mexican youth had been incarcerated, compared to not a single Chinese or Korean second-generation immigrant.

Some "segmented assimilation" theorists argue that while the second generation advances in relation to their parents, many immigrant parents start at extremely low levels of education and employment, and certain groups have substantial rates of arrest, incarceration, early child-bearing and other indicia of downward assimilation (Haller, Portes, and Lynch 2011, 757).

144

Others emphasize the "modest upward mobility" of the second generation, as evidenced by their fluency in English, decreased concentrations in "immigrant" jobs, and the occupation of a shared "social and economic space" with native-born whites and native-born minorities (Alba, Kasinitz and Waters 2011, 766).

The sociologist Tomás Jimenéz has concluded that integration is "proceeding steadily, but unevenly," with Latino(a)s progressing less rapidly than Asians, black and non-Hispanic whites with immigrant backgrounds (Jimenéz 2011, 18). However, the literature does not validate concerns that certain populations cannot be integrated or that immigrants overall are integrating at a slower pace than did prior generations. At the same time, the second and third generations in certain communities face a heightened risk of downward assimilation.[2]

Jimenéz considered five indicia of integration: language proficiency; socioeconomic attainment; political participation; residential segregation; and interaction with host communities. He found that:

- Recent immigrants are "learning English faster" than those who arrived in the late nineteenth and early twentieth century: 75 percent of immigrants who arrived between 1980 and 2000 spoke English well or very well within five years, compared to less than one-half who arrived between 1900 and 1920.
- By the third generation, nearly "everyone, regardless of ethno-racial group, reports speaking English well or very well."

---

2   This finding heightens a longstanding concern of the US bishops that standard Catholic youth ministries do not "fit" second- and third-generation Latino(a) youth (USCCB 2002).

- The second generation in all ethnoracial groups fares better than the first generation "on all measures of socio-economic progress," including educational attainment, income, occupational status, and homeownership.
- Second generation Latino(a)s do not reach parity with US-born non-Hispanic whites, despite "dramatic improvement over the first generation" and "signs of dramatic progress" on poverty and homeownership.
- Immigrant residential segregation decreases from the first to second generation, but Hispanic segregation exceeds that of Asians.
- Naturalization numbers rose dramatically from the 1970s to 2008 and remain high, though large numbers of naturalization-eligible LPRs have not naturalized.
- Ethno-racial and national groups inter-marry at rising rates over time, although Hispanics have lower inter-marriage rates in all generations than Asians (ibid., 5, 7, 9-10, 12-13,15).

Another study used census data on arrivals in the 1970s, 1980s, 1990s, and 2000s to project integration outcomes by 2030 in English proficiency, homeownership, education levels, earnings and naturalization (Myers and Pitkin 2011). The study projected that by 2030, the great majority of arrivals in the 1990s would speak English well, own their homes, complete high school, naturalize, live out of poverty, and earn better than a low income.

These studies provide mostly positive news on immigrant integration. However, they also illustrate the need for a multi-generational commitment to integration; for the removal of barriers to integration like lack of immigration status and inability to access services; and for Catholic institutions to mobilize their moral and material resources in support of at-risk youth.

2. INTEGRATION AND THE FUTURE OF THE CATHOLIC CHURCH IN THE UNITED STATES

Recent surveys of US residents on religion, immigration, national identity and culture illustrate the convergence between the vitality and needs of immigrant communities, and the mission and resources of Catholic institutions.[3] Their findings relate primarily but not exclusively to Hispanics, the largest ethnic group, and to non-Hispanic whites.

First, they highlight the growing influence, importance and vitality of Latino(a)s and immigrants to US society and to the Catholic Church, given their expanding numbers and their youth. A 2013 analysis of the US Catholic population by race, ethnicity and country of birth found that Hispanics represented 38 percent of US Catholics; Asian, Native Hawaiian, and Pacific Islanders 4 percent; and non-Hispanic black, African-American, African, and (non-Hispanic) Afro-Caribbean 3 percent (Gray et al. 2013, 9).[4]

Hispanics alone make up 38 percent of all US Catholics, 58 percent of Catholics between ages 18 and 34 (Millennials), and

---

3   These surveys include the 2006 "Faith Matters" survey of 3,108 Americans, conducted on behalf of Harvard University's John F. Kennedy School of Government and summarized by Robert Putnam and David Campbell in *American Grace: How Religion Divides and Unites Us*; a 2006 survey of 4,016 persons of Latino(a) background or descent for the Pew Forum on Religion and Public Life and the Pew Hispanic Center; the 2008 "Religious Landscape Survey" by the Pew Forum of 35,556 US adults; and a 2013 survey of 4,465 US adults by the Public Religion Research Institute (PRRI). The PRRI survey, in partnership with the Brookings Institution, covered immigration policy, national identity, culture and religious values. Respondents included 938 Catholics, among them 647 white Catholics, 211 Hispanic Catholics, and 80 "other non-white Catholics," including Asian, black non-Hispanic and other/mixed. Most recently, the Pew Research Center surveyed 5,103 Hispanic adults from May 24 to July 28, 2013.

4   Fifty-one percent of Hispanic Catholics are foreign born, compared to five percent of white Catholics (PRRI 2013).

67 percent of Millennials who regularly attend mass (Gray et al. 2013). Over the next 30 years, the number of second-generation Hispanics will double and the number of third-generation Hispanics will triple (Matovina 2012, 222). Seventy-one percent of Hispanic Catholics and 58 percent of other non-white Catholics fall within the 18 to 29 or the 30 to 49 age cohorts (PRRI 2013). By way of comparison, 67 percent of white Catholics fall within the age 50 to 64 or the 65 and above cohorts (ibid.).[5]

More than 40 percent of whites with Catholic parents have either switched religion or no longer identify with any religion, and nearly 45 percent of white Catholics rarely attend mass (Putnam and Campbell 2010, 138). Yet despite this low "retention" rate, the Catholic share of the US population has remained at roughly 25 percent due primarily to the inflow of Latino(a) Catholics (ibid., 299-300).

Fifty-nine percent of persons who self-identify as Hispanic are Catholic, including 67 percent of the Hispanic foreign-born (Gray et al. 2013, 7). Sixty-five percent of Filipinos and 26 percent of African immigrants are Catholic (ibid.) However, recent polling has found falling rates of Catholicism among Hispanics, and lower rates of Catholicism among Hispanic youth than among older cohorts. A 2013 survey of 5,103 Hispanic adults by the Pew Research Center, for example, found that 55 percent of US Latino(a)s identify as Catholic, including 60 percent of foreign-born Latino(a)s (Pew Research Center 2014, 29, 31). However, only 45 percent of 18 to 29-year-old Latino(a)s identify as Catholic, compared to 57 percent of 30 to 40 year olds and 64 percent of those aged 50 or above (ibid., 9).

---

5   Another study found that 45 percent of Catholics under the age of 30 were Hispanic, and that 85 percent of Catholics over age 70 were white (The Pew Forum 2008, 36).

Parishes represent another vantage point on the growing importance of Latino(a)s and other immigrant groups to the Catholic Church in the United States. A national survey of Catholic parishes in 2010 found that Latino(a)s accounted for 40 percent of the growth in registered parishioners between 2005 and 2010 (Gray, Gautier and Cidade 2011, 4-5). Over the same period, the proportion of non-Hispanic white parishioners decreased, while registered Latino(a), Asian, and Pacific Islanders grew, particularly in multi-cultural parishes (ibid., 54).

Twenty-nine percent of US parishes report celebrating mass at least once a month in a language other than English, up from 22 percent in 2000 (Gray, Gautier and Cidade 2011, 31). In addition, 37 percent of parishes report having special observances for cultural or ethnic groups and 21 percent celebrate the Feast Day of Our Lady of Guadalupe (ibid., 34).

Figure I: US Parishes that Celebrate Mass at Least Once a Month in a Language Other Than English

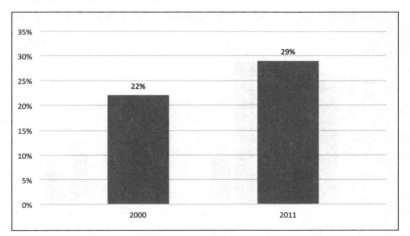

Source: Gray, Gautier and Cidade 2011, 31.

149

Figure J: US Parishes that Celebrate Special Observances and the Feast Day of Our Lady of Guadalupe

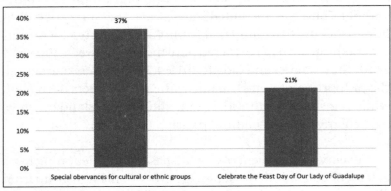

Source: Gray, Gautier and Cidade 2011, 34.

Perhaps most dramatically, the number of infant/child baptisms (by parish) exceed funerals by far higher rates in the ethnically and racially diverse South (79.4 to 24.6) and West (93.1 to 31.2), than in the Northeast (47.2 to 42.4) and Midwest (34.6 to 22) (ibid., 6-7, 37).

Figure K: Average Number of Infant/Child Baptisms and Funerals by Parish

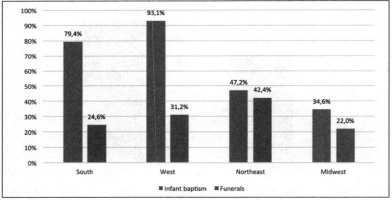

Source: Gray, Gautier and Cidade 2011, 6-7.

Second, a related and perhaps under-reported phenomenon is the optimism of Hispanic Catholics, which is consistent with the optimism of first generation immigrants overall (Alba, Kasinitz and Waters 2011, 764). Hispanic Catholics express higher levels of satisfaction than white Catholics with the "way things are going" in the country (46 to 25 percent) (PRRI 2013), and greater optimism regarding the effect of change and the nation's direction (Figure L).

Figure L: Greater Optimism of Hispanic Catholics

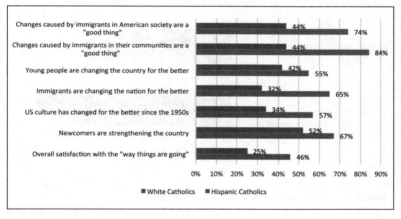

Source: Public Religion Research Institute 2013.

Third, Hispanics "demonstrate high commitments to the Christian faith and to traditional concepts of family," and foreign-born Hispanics "are often more socially, spiritually, and politically conservative" than other Hispanics (Barna: Hispanics 2013). Hispanic Catholics hold views that more closely align with church teaching than their white co-religionists on divorce, abortion, premarital sex, women priests, the death penalty, and support for the Catholic hierarchy (Putnam and Campbell 2010, 302; The Pew Forum 2007, 69, 72). Fifty-six

151

percent of white Catholics think abortion should be legal in all or most cases, compared to 47 percent of Hispanic Catholics (PRRI 2013). The exception to this overall finding is that Hispanics oppose same-sex marriage at lower rates than white Catholics (The Pew Forum 2007, 69; PRRI 2013). Forty-two percent of Hispanic Catholics highly prioritize addressing the "moral breakdown" of the United States, compared to 28 percent of whites.

Figure M: Views on Abortion and "Moral Breakdown"

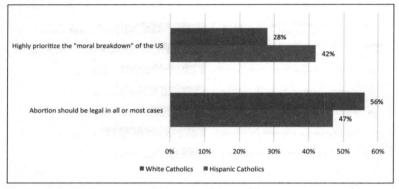

Source: Public Religion Research Institute 2013.

Hispanic Catholics also value socio-economic justice at high levels. Eighty-six percent believe the government should work to reduce income disparities between rich and poor, and 87 percent say the government should devote more resources to assist the poor, compared to 61 and 40 percent respectively of white Catholics (Putman and Campbell 2010, 303-304). Likewise, Hispanic Catholics believe at higher rates than white Catholics and persons in other religious traditions, that the government bears primary responsibility for caring for the poor (ibid., 257). Sixty-five percent of Hispanic Catholics believe that the poor have "hard lives due to lack of government services," compared to 52 percent of white Catholics (The Pew Forum 2007, 73).

Fourth, the surveys reveal a church with substantial percentages of members on both ends of the socio-economic spectrum. Thirty-one percent of Catholics live in families with annual incomes of less than $30,000 and 19 percent live in families with incomes of more than $100,000 (The Pew Forum 2008, 78). These figures are comparable to the national figures.

The survey conducted by the Public Religion Research Institute (PRRI) also found that 63 percent of Hispanic Catholics have a high school education or less, compared to 33 percent of white Catholics and 36 percent of other non-white Catholics (PRRI 2013).

Figure N: Catholics with High School Education or Less

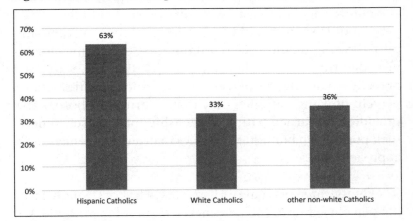

Source: Public Religion Research Institute 2013.

Fifth, Hispanic Catholics receive substantial support from their churches, but significantly lower levels of certain forms of

153

support than Hispanics in other religious traditions. Hispanic Catholics report that their church helps them with financial problems (58 percent), finding a job (52 percent), child care (52 percent), and finding housing (45 percent), but these rates are lower than for Hispanics in other religious traditions (The Pew Forum 2007, 23). However, Catholic churches provide members with food or clothing (83 percent) and language or literacy training (57 percent) at roughly the same rates as non-Catholic churches (ibid.).

3. Catholics and Immigration Reform

The US immigration reform debate has received widespread attention in recent years. The PRRI survey demonstrates broad support, including among Catholics, for three prongs of comprehensive immigration reform: a path to citizenship for the unauthorized; reform of the laws governing legal admission; and enforcement of the law. Sixty-five percent of Catholics (74 percent of Hispanics and 62 percent of whites) say they support allowing unauthorized immigrants "to become citizens provided they meet certain criteria" (PRRI 2013). Sixty-nine percent—including 82 percent of Hispanic Catholics and 63 percent of white Catholics—say that securing the border and providing an earned path to citizenship more closely reflects their position on immigration policy than an enforcement-only approach (ibid.).

Eighty-three percent of Hispanic Catholics strongly favor (33 percent) or favor (50 percent) elements of the DREAM Act. In contrast, 55 percent of white Catholics strongly favor (14 percent) or favor (41 percent) the DREAM Act (ibid.).

Figure O: Catholic Support for the DREAM Act

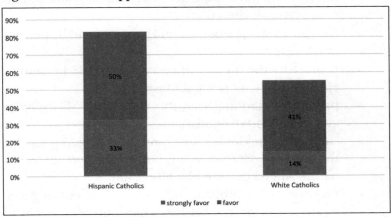

Source: Public Religion Research Institute 2013.

Seventy-eight percent of Catholics (92 percent Hispanic, 71 percent white) favor allowing immigrants who obtain degrees from US colleges or universities in math, science or technology to work legally in the United States. Seventy-five percent (87 percent Hispanics and 69 percent whites) favor an expanded "guest worker" programs that would provide temporary visas to non-citizens who want to work legally in the United States. Sixty-four percent (71 percent of Hispanics, and 62 percent of whites) mostly or completely disagreed that the best way to resolve "illegal" immigration is to make life so difficult for unauthorized immigrants that they will be forced to return home. Fifty-nine percent (78 percent of Hispanics and 49 percent of white Catholics) mostly or completely disagree that the United States should make a serious effort to deport all "illegal" immigrants (PRRI 2013).

PRRI also found substantial alignment between white and Hispanic Catholics on the values that should guide immigration reform. Among the values identified as extremely or very important were:

155

- family unification (95 percent of Hispanics and 80 percent of whites agreed);
- the rule of law (85 percent of Hispanics and 81 percent of whites);
- protecting the dignity of every person (83 percent of Hispanics and 82 percent of whites);
- promoting national security (86 percent of Hispanics and 91 percent of whites);
- "following the Golden Rule" and providing immigrants the same opportunity as "my family" (78 percent of Hispanics and 65 percent of whites); and
- following the biblical example of welcoming the stranger (59 percent of Hispanics and 40 percent of whites).[6]

Figure P: Values That Should Guide Immigration Reform

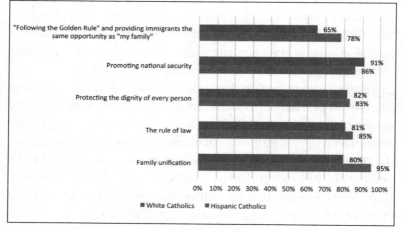

Source: Public Religion Research Institute 2013.

---

6   The relatively low percentage of respondents who identified "welcoming the stranger" as an "important" or "extremely important" value is likely due to the negative secular connotations of the word "stranger."

156

Hispanic and white Catholics, however, express disparate views on migration-related labor and economic issues. Thirty-five percent of whites said that immigrants mostly take jobs away from American citizens, compared to 11 percent of Hispanics. Eighty-two percent of Hispanics say that immigrants mostly take jobs Americans do not want, compared to 59 percent of whites. Sixty-seven percent of Hispanics say that "illegal immigrants" mostly help the economy by providing low-cost labor, compared to 32 percent of whites. Sixty-one percent of whites say that immigrants mostly hurt the economy by driving down wages, compared to 30 percent of Hispanics (PRRI 2013).

White and Hispanic Catholics also differ significantly on the persons who should be given "preference" in the US immigration system. English language acquisition can be a flash point in immigration debates, but it is not a requirement that Hispanics resist. To the contrary, a significantly higher percent of Hispanics than whites (61 to 43 percent) say the US immigration laws should give preference to fluent English speakers.

Hispanics also supported (at higher rates than whites) affording preference to persons with children or parents living legally in the United States (79 to 57 percent) and to persons with a spouse living in the United States legally (71 to 63 percent). Seventy-four percent of Hispanics say that persons with a degree from a US college or university should be given preference, compared to 56 percent of whites. Forty-four percent of Hispanics say that preference should be given to persons with a gay or lesbian spouse living in the United States legally, compared to 25 percent of white Catholics. Forty-four percent of Hispanics, compared to 27 percent of whites, say that preference should be given to persons from Western Europe (PRRI 2013).

4. Catholics, Immigration and the Challenge of Unity

Many Catholic politicians have embraced "self-deportation" or attrition-through-enforcement policies in an attempt to make life so difficult for unauthorized immigrants and their families that they will be forced leave. Some propose immigration policies rooted in population control or other concerns that find little support in Catholic teaching. Others fund think-tanks that favor substantial reductions in immigration, regularly attack the US bishops, and offer "alternative" faith voices that embrace restrictionist agendas.[7]

Some Catholic intellectuals and policymakers treat church teaching on migrants and newcomers as a kind of second-tier priority and dismiss the US bishops' policy positions in this area as a matter of "prudential judgment." Many Catholic institutions, including those whose vitality depends on attracting newcomers, aggressively defend Catholic teaching on other issues, but rarely speak against anti-immigrant rhetoric.

Others harshly criticize the bishops (Appleby 2013, 297-298). A 2013 piece on immigration reform by the editor of the Faith and Reason Institute's journal *The Catholic Thing* provides a case in point. It portrays the US bishops as partly principled, but mostly as cynical, dissembling, political operatives (Miner 2013). The author deigns to "suspect" that the US bishops might be motivated, in part, by "Christian compassion" over "the plight

---

7   One commentator, for example, has argued in favor of prioritizing visas for persons who promise "*not* to have children" (North 2011). Under his "dream" proposal, such persons would be required to "sign a formal agreement with the government saying that if they become a birth parent they would lose their right to be in America, that they know that they will be removed from the nation immediately and that they would have no recourse to the courts on this matter" (ibid.).

of Central American immigrants."[8] However, he also accuses the bishops of engaging in a "baldly political" exercise, claims (incorrectly) that they support "open borders," calls them "scofflaws," and charges them with advocating for reform based on "a desire to ... bolster demographics in America's flagging dioceses" (ibid.). One would expect faithful Catholics to defend the bishops' moral authority and good-faith. Yet these *ad hominem* attacks impugn the integrity of the bishops and are rife with substantive errors. Moreover, they issue with regularity from Catholic politicians and certain Catholic institutions, including those that tout their faithfulness to the church. They demonstrate why "communion" will require effective evangelization of many natives.

---

8   The author presumably includes Mexico in Central America.

V. Making Integration a Unifying, Institutional Priority

This book argues that the Catholic Church in the United States should make immigrant integration a unifying, institutional priority in keeping with its theological self-understanding, its mission, and its identity as a church of immigrants. It sets forth a Catholic vision of integration that places political participation, socio-economic advancement and the cultural metrics of integration within a broad framework of human flourishing, integral development, and communion based on universal values.

It identifies the over-arching conditions that have allowed immigrants, their children and grandchildren to integrate in the United States, including an open labor market, family-based immigration policies, a participatory political system, a robust civil society, and Constitutional rights that apply to persons, not just citizens. The Catholic Church in the United States, in collaboration with other institutions, must ensure that these conditions are safeguarded and honored on a federal, state, and local level.[1]

---

1   Of course, the church should work to identify and strengthen core "integrating" conditions, and to strengthen ties between migrant- sending and -receiving communities.

The status quo of 11.7 million unauthorized residents, record deportations, and millions of divided families does not honor these principles. Legal status is a pre-condition to full integration. However, integration goes well beyond and need not wait for legislative reform. The lives of immigrants and their children can be stabilized, regularized and improved even without federal legislation through state and local laws and policies that provide immigrants with access to post-secondary education, drivers' licenses, identification cards, public services, and police protection.

In his Apostolic Exhortation *Evangelii Gaudium (EG)*, Pope Francis summoned the church to be "permanently in a state of mission" (*EG* 25). He cautioned that the parish, in particular, should not become a "a useless structure out of touch with people or a self-absorbed group made up of a chosen few" (28). "I dream of a 'missionary option,'" he wrote, "capable of transforming everything, so that the Church's customs, ways of doing things, times and schedules, languages and structures can be suitably channeled for the evangelization of today's world rather than for her self-preservation" (27).

This book queries whether Catholic institutions can become, in Pope Francis's words, "environments of living communion and participation" and "completely mission oriented" (28). It seeks to initiate a process within the church –reflected in a growing web of commitments, partnerships and initiatives— that fosters the leadership and initiative of immigrants. It highlights several elements that will be vital to a successful initiative. These include the need to:

- Educate Catholics in their own faith tradition, their membership in a church of immigrants, and on *why* they should make integration (communion) a priority.

- Create institutions and pastoral models that allow immigrants to sustain their cultural practices and means of religious expression.
- Reform laws and public policies that impede integration, and support pro-integration policies that reflect Catholic teaching.
- Promote the good of both natives and newcomers and foster "a culture of solidarity" that crosses borders.
- Ensure that government funding does not inhibit Catholic institutions from addressing the structural causes of poverty and injustice.
- Honor popular religious and cultural traditions as part of a larger vision of promoting unity through diversity.
- Retain strong ties to long-settled Catholics, but reorient Catholic institutions in light of the church's mission to gather together God's scattered children and to serve those in need.
- Cultivate the initiative, leadership and gifts of lay persons, particularly those from immigrant communities.
- Develop creative funding strategies that substantially expand services and ministries to heavily immigrant communities.
- Revisit and rejuvenate ministries that were essential to previous generations of immigrants and their progeny.

The book has identified successful initiatives that could form the basis of a larger Catholic commitment to integration. It seeks to inspire Catholic institutions to adapt, internalize and concretize the animating Catholic vision of integral development and communion. It calls for the diverse networks of Catholic institutions to assess how they can best contribute to a unified approach to immigrant well-being. Distinct intra-network dialogues will be necessary given the diversity of Catholic institutions, populations served and operating environments. At

163

the same time, these separate assessments must be connected to a set of broader conversations on how Catholic institutions can collectively contribute to communion between natives and newcomers. While it would be premature to anticipate the results of these dialogues, several challenges will confront Catholic institutions if they prioritize integration.

First, they will need to develop a collective response due to the size, diversity, and immense needs of immigrant communities, and the church's ambitious vision of integration. The church seeks to evangelize both native and immigrant cultures, to create the conditions that allow all persons to flourish, to build communion based on shared values, and to promote integral development. These goals cannot be met without the full and coordinated commitment of the church's defining institutions, as well as extensive partnerships with public and other private entities. Because integration occurs over generations and US immigration levels show few signs of abating, the church should make a long-term commitment to this challenge. On a programmatic level, facilitating integration requires the integration of diverse services and programs.

Second, the Catholic Church will need to draw on the talents, leadership and resources of immigrant communities. Catholic institutions can realize their potential as mediating and integrating entities only if they fully incorporate immigrants, their children and grandchildren. They must model openness themselves. Catholic teaching does not view newcomers as persons to "plan for" or "passive recipients of the church's mission" (Groody 2007, 184; USCCB 2002, 44), but as agents in their own lives and potential leaders of Catholic institutions. Moreover, ensuring the "full participation" of immigrants "in the church and society with equal rights and duties continues the biblical understanding of the justice of God reaching out to all peoples and rectifying the situation of the poor, the orphans, the widows, the disadvantaged, and especially in the Old Testament, the alien and the stranger" (NCCB 1986). Thus, a cross-cutting goal of this initiative should be the full integration of immigrants into the life of Catholic institutions. This represents a substantial challenge for the Catholic Church in the United States, but also an historic opportunity for self-renewal.

Participation may seem a self-evident, pre-condition to "communion," but it will not occur easily or automatically. It will require substantial leadership and initiative and will face resistance. Some native parishioners, for example, argue that the celebration of mass in the native languages of immigrants risks creating "parishes within parishes" and provides a disincentive to English language acquisition (Odem 2004, 36). Others complain—as nativists have persistently done in the past—that immigrants do not sufficiently contribute to church coffers.[2] Some parishes relegate immigrants to advisory committees, rather than including them in canonically recognized parish councils. Low parish "registration" rates by immigrants have also been a source of tension.

Third, immigrants will understandably search for spiritual communities that accept, understand and actively support them, whether Catholic or not (USCCB 2008, 11; Pew Research Center 2014, 42). The decline in the number of vowed religious makes mission-driven, lay leaders and staffing—particularly from members of immigrant and minority communities—all the more essential to the success of Catholic institutions. Moreover, as it did in the past, the church should promote the integral development of immigrants, their children and grandchildren

---

2   One study found that immigrants volunteer extensively and donate heavily to sacramental and other celebrations (Hoover 2014, 61, 166).

by working with them to establish an exhaustive and responsive network of services, ministries and institutions.

Integration begins with the hopes, aspirations and dreams of immigrants. The concept of "communion" underscores the agency and the social nature of human beings. In Catholic teaching, human beings become themselves in service to God and to each other (Hoover 2014, 198). In turning to Catholic (and other) institutions to "mediate" the larger society, immigrants "journey," find their place "within a community," and realize their dignity (*Lumen Fidei* 14). The church cannot serve this role if immigrants and their children cannot access or do not feel a sense of ownership or homecoming in Catholic institutions.

Fourth, Catholic institutions should prioritize the needs of second- and third-generation youth and young adults. The health and vitality of the church and nation will be increasingly tied to the success of the rapidly growing second and third generation. Youth and young adults, in particular, represent a potential source of leadership and activism, and an entry point into immigrant families and communities. However, they face the pressures of bridging multiple cultures and the risk of assimilation into the negative features of host communities. They represent a distinct cultural group from their immigrant parents, neither completely American nor members of their ancestral nation, pulled between their parents' culture and the "impact of American culture through the school, the streets, and the media" (Fitzpatrick 1987, 160). For these reasons, there is a pressing need to minister to youth who do not fit into typical youth ministries (USCCB 2002). The challenge will be to guide youth towards a "cultural manifestation of their faith" that builds on the positive values of US culture and the cultures of their communities of origin (Fitzpatrick 1987, 161). If the Catholic Church fails in this task, it risks losing the future (ibid.).

A values-based vision of "communion" would prioritize the well-being and catechesis of immigrant youth through parishes, schools, youth programs, and other ministries. It would affirm the positive values found in the (often) multi-cultural homes and communities of immigrants, and fortify them against the distortions and excesses of US popular culture.

Fifth, Catholic institutions cannot promote integration in the thick sense of communion grounded in shared beliefs and values, if they do not communicate their values. It cannot be assumed that the stakeholders in Catholic institutions—board members, staff, volunteers, community leaders and beneficiaries—will invariably understand the touchstones of these institutions. Compounding this challenge, secular and other faith-based institutions provide similar services, clients come from diverse faith traditions (or from none at all), and many Catholics are not literate in their own tradition. The question arises: how to communicate Catholic identity and values in ways that immigrant and native populations understand?

Catholic institutions struggle unevenly with this challenge. A 2006 study comparing faith-based refugee resettlement agencies, with secular resettlement agencies (Mutual Assistance Agencies or "MAAs") rooted in particular ethnic communities found that "faith-based NGOs [nongovernmental organizations] use religion as a motivation and rationale for the almost completely secular services they provide to refugees" (Nawyn 2006, 1516-1519). Moreover, while faith-based organizations developed more relationships with local religious institutions, they encouraged religious practice *less* frequently than MAAs (ibid.). In addition, MAAs engaged in more "religious" activities because they sought to build "community," while faith-based agencies focused more narrowly on the government resettlement objective of securing early self-sufficiency through employment (1522-1524).

167

Similarly, a study of the refugee resettlement work of Catholic Charities of Los Angeles found that the archdiocese had offered a Catholic rationale for initially accepting federal resettlement funding; i.e., to empower local communities consistent with the principle of subsidiarity. Catholic Charities leadership also continued to locate this work within a broader religious vision, including respect for the dignity and diverse beliefs of clients. However, the study found that employees providing services framed their work "as a non-religious functional domain and, therefore, presumptively secular in both discourse and service" (Bruce 2006, 1494, 1501). In effect, staff who related to refugees and immigrants on a day-to-day basis viewed the agency's religious identity as "most appropriately voiced" by agency leadership, and agency leadership left it to ground-level employees to articulate their work in secular terms, consistent with grant requirements (ibid., 1504).

Pope Benedict XVI urged Catholic institutions to remain "credible witnesses to Christ" and to avoid becoming "just another form of social assistance" (*DCE* 31). At the same time, Catholic teaching prohibits conditioning service to persons in need on the basis on their religious convictions, much less their willingness to submit to proselytization (ibid.). Nor is such a practice permitted under the ethical tenets that guide humanitarian work or the conditions of federal funding. In short, "evangelization" of culture may be more the explicit domain of parishes and pastoral ministries than of service agencies.

On the other hand, Catholic institutions need to define and communicate what makes them Catholic with greater rigor. The maxim that the church serves the poor not because "they are Catholic," but because "we are Catholic," speaks powerfully to its vision of human dignity, but not to why or how it should do its work or what it ultimately hopes to accomplish. It also assumes a level of catechesis that most Catholics have not received and a level of familiarity with Catholic teaching that many do not possess.

Catholic institutions must honor the diverse religions and cultures of those they serve, but also internalize and communicate their own tradition. It cannot be assumed that the boards, leaders, and staff of Catholic institutions come to their positions with the necessary level of knowledge or clarity on these issues. Nor can it be assumed that Catholic institutions, individually and collectively, have prioritized "formation of the heart" (*DCE* 31(a)), or engaged the hard issues of how to build community in light of Gospel values. This challenge requires an ongoing commitment to educate the boards, leadership, staff, volunteers, clients, and the broader public. It also requires that Catholic institutions serve populations and meet human needs that go beyond those that are valued or funded by the government.

In CLINIC's early years, its then director (one of the authors) struggled to find guidance or a template for what made Catholic agencies different from other agencies that competently served the poor. CLINIC's board of directors eventually developed and adopted a statement on Catholic identity, which served as a touchstone for its decisions on which populations to serve, partnerships to pursue, and programs to offer. The agency subsequently made it a priority to feature Catholic teaching in its staff orientation, annual network gatherings, publications and web-site. While not a template for other Catholic institutions, the statement represented CLINIC's attempt to discern and own what makes it a Catholic agency. It reads:

> CLINIC's Catholic identity infuses every aspect of its work—how it is governed, who it serves, how it treats its clients, the way it works, and why it does the work that it does. First, CLINIC is a sub-

sidiary of the US Conference of Catholic Bishops and is governed by a Board comprised primarily of bishops. It operates as a legal support agency for diocesan immigration programs. Second, the kinds of cases and advocacy positions taken by the Catholic network—involving family reunification, protection of the persecuted, empowerment through work authorization, legal status and citizenship—have their roots in Catholic social teaching. Third, CLINIC views newcomers in their full human dignity, not solely from a legal service perspective. This requires CLINIC and its affiliates to partner with programs and agencies that can meet the non-legal needs of newcomers. Fourth, CLINIC takes the Catholic view that advocacy draws its legitimacy from service. Service allows advocates to give voice to newcomers, not to speak "for" them. Fifth, CLINIC has adopted a principle of Catholic social teaching—subsidiarity—to guide its programmatic commitments. Subsidiarity leads CLINIC to respect the different roles and capacities of its local partner agencies and to encourage them to assume as much responsibility for newcomers as they can. This allows CLINIC to focus its limited resources on needs that local programs cannot meet. In this way, CLINIC seeks to leverage maximum legal representation for low-income newcomers. Sixth, the Catholic network safeguards the rights and promotes the dignity of all newcomers; it does not distinguish among prospective clients based on race, religion or ethnic background.

Sixth, Catholic agencies need to invest in establishing, documenting and sharing best practices, including through meetings of Catholic agency heads and staff from diverse institutions. At this writing, Catholic institutions have mobilized to serve the record number of unaccompanied children and parents with children from Mexico and Central America who fled violence and privation and entered the United States in 2014. Yet the church's extraordinary response—in providing shelter, and family unity, legal, pastoral, health and social services—has been poorly documented and has received far less attention than a handful of protests against the settlement of the children in particular communities. Nor have its successful service-delivery and pastoral models been disseminated throughout the Catholic community or outside it. Catholic institutions would be more influential in the public sphere and better equipped to carry out their missions if they systematically shared and publicized their work. Their institutions, programs and ministries to immigrants would also benefit immensely from greater attention by researchers and scholars.

Funding is another neuralgic challenge in many Catholic institutions and a particular barrier to increasing immigrant and minority enrollment in Catholic schools. This book outlines three models for addressing this need. In 2013, the Archdiocese of Los Angeles' Catholic Education Foundation awarded $16.2 million in tuition assistance to 11,800 students at the federal poverty line and qualifying for free or reduced lunches (CEF 2013, 4). Since 1987, CEF has provided more than $136 million in tuition assistance (ibid). The Cristo Rey network has developed a unique program that simultaneously helps to cover tuition costs and provide students with experience in the workplace. The Segura Initiative charges tuition based on ability to pay, supplemented by scholarships, and it encourages in-kind contributions by parents.

The financial viability of heavily Hispanic parishes and the establishment of parishes in communities with large minority and immigrant populations may well require new models and sources of funding, given understandably lower offertory giving in these communities (Ospino 2014a, 42).

Seventh, an initiative to improve and expand the integration work of Catholic institutions would require short- and long-term integration goals and metrics by individual institution, institutional sectors, and across different Catholic sectors. The process of establishing appropriate goals and metrics would ensure greater accountability within and collaboration between diverse Catholic institutions.

As it stands, many Catholic institutions do not track their services (outputs) to immigrant populations, much less the integration "outcomes" of such services. In some cases, as with Catholic hospitals, this is part of a deliberate decision not to collect information that might dissuade immigrants from using vitally necessary services. In other cases, Catholic institutions track narrow integration metrics to reflect funder demands and grant requirements. Refugee resettlement programs, for example, measure early employment outcomes, but do not assess refugee integration in a broader sense or over the long-term. Some projects, like the Notre Dame Task Force on the Participation of Latino(a) Children and Families in Catholic Schools, have established overarching enrollment goals for an entire category of institutions.

The Migration Integration Policy Index assesses the integration performance of 31 European and North American nations based on indicators and detailed metrics that cover labor market mobility, family reunification, education, political participation, long-term residence, access to nationality, and anti-discrimination laws and policies (Huddleston et al., 2011). The University of Southern California's Center for the Study of Immigrant Integration has developed an integration scorecard to measure state and regional integration policies against four categories of indicators: current economic status; economic mobility over time; the openness of receiving communities; and civic participation (Pastor et al. 2012). Similarly, Catholic institutions should develop indicators, metrics and scorecards for the integration of immigrants that they serve. Just as importantly, they should develop integration metrics that speak to the leadership, staffing and accessibility of Catholic institutions.

Eighth, the church needs to educate Catholics on its identity and history as a church of immigrants. The rapid growth of the US immigrant populations has led to tensions, fears, and a sense of displacement on the part of some natives, including Catholics. Many argue that immigrants do not wish to integrate or that they present an economic and cultural threat. Others distinguish between their own ancestors and today's unauthorized immigrants. Yet the concept of "illegal immigrants" did not come into being until the national origin quota legislation in 1924, which created the first categorical limits on legal immigration and were intended to exclude (mostly Catholic) southern and eastern Europeans.[3] Some inaccurately claim that immigrants commit crimes and receive public benefits at higher rates than natives.[4] Others argue that today's (heavily Catholic) immigrant populations cannot be integrated due to their size, supposedly divided loyalties, and lack of proficiency in English. Earlier generations of US Catholics endured the same unfounded suspicions.

The church should address these issues directly, particularly at the parish level. Only 23 percent of white Catholics report that their clergy often or sometimes speak on immigration (PRRI 2013). This is a glaring omission given Christ's radical identification with the stranger and the central Christian insight that salvation depends on empathy, hospitality and love of the migrant. Moreover, it does not require great erudition or courage to preach on the church's biblical history of exodus, exile and dispersion; Christ's identification with migrants; the

---

3   By the late nineteenth century, Congress had also introduced the concept of inadmissibility, prohibiting the entry of certain immigrants and, by extension, creating categories of unauthorized persons.

4   However, Catholic immigrants were "heavily overrepresented on the relief rolls and in the correctional institutions of American cities" in the early twentieth century (Brown and McKeown 1997, 51).

spread of Christianity; or the immigrant roots of the Catholic Church in the United States. There is hardly a biblical story or parable that does not involve migrants or migration. To locate immigrants within a continuous American and Catholic saga can promote empathy from natives and instill in immigrants a sense of belonging.

Pastors and other church leaders should also create fora in which immigrants, their children and grandchildren can speak to their co-religionists on their hopes, aspirations, and needs. Integration requires that natives "risk being changed" by newcomers and persons of different cultures (USCCB 2002). Thus, one pastoral challenge will be to provide natives with more exposure to immigrants and the immigrant experience. As it stands, 44 percent of white Catholics report having no close friends born outside the United States. In addition, a significant percentage of US Catholics have lost a sense of their own immigrant histories (PRRI 2013).

Immigrants are overwhelmingly hard-working, family- and community-oriented, and strong of faith. As in the past, many endure low wages and dangerous working conditions, and their families face substantial challenges and strain, often to the breaking point. Communion requires community members to understand and to respond to the needs of their near and far neighbors. The Catholic Church will not be able to build unity between immigrants and natives based on the shared values embedded in their diverse cultures if these groups do not relate and (ultimately) empathize with each other.

Ninth, the book recognizes the need to evangelize and reorient individual Catholics and Catholic institutions. It has described promising and successful integration programs. Yet immigrants and their children remain "invisible" to many Catholic institutions (USCCB 2008, 22). Some immigrant leaders express disappointment over what they perceive to be the apathy and indifference of "the church" towards their communities. Other Catholic institutions have actively opposed the US bishops' public policy initiatives for immigration reform in the most derisive terms. The church needs to develop a collective strategy to engage Catholics who ignore or dissent from its teaching on immigration. The ability to facilitate integration depends, in part, on the evangelization of these Catholics. In any event, Catholics with diverse positions on immigration policy—and, in particular, on how to address "illegal immigration"—should be able to coalesce in support of stronger, unified communities based on shared values.

The book has used the term "leaders" to refer to persons within the church hierarchy, religious communities, and diverse institutions. Yet Catholic leaders, defined in this way, operate within a larger society in which Catholics represent the single largest religious community and have assumed prominence in government, business, labor unions, education, health care and other sectors that would have been unthinkable a century ago. Well-established residents could contribute significantly to the expansion and improvement of the church's institutional commitments to immigrants. They could also expand integration opportunities for immigrants within their spheres of influence. Immigrant integration cannot become a unifying priority without the active support of both natives and newcomers.

One of the enduring myths about the Catholic Church is that it operates in a top-down, lock-step, near military style. Of course, the church's work with immigrants depends on strong leadership and guidance from the Holy See and US bishops. It also rests on the formal commitments of its established institutions and communities.[5] Just as importantly, however, it depends on countless smaller communities of faith, inspiration and leadership. The church acts when "two or more are gathered" in His name (Mt. 18:20), and integration happens on the level of individuals, families and communities. In Catholic terms, immigrant integration cannot become a Catholic priority unless the pockets of "faith, hope and charity" that form the "Mystical Body of Christ" make it one (*LG* 8).

---

5   More precisely, it depends on the initiative and devotion of *individuals* within these structures and communities.

Appendix A

US Foreign-Born Population by Nation of Origin

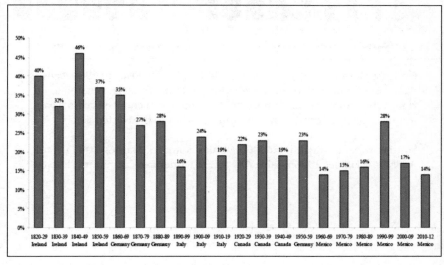

Source: US Department of Homeland Security 2012 (Table 2).

US Foreign-Born Population by Nation of Origin: 1850-2010 – Europe

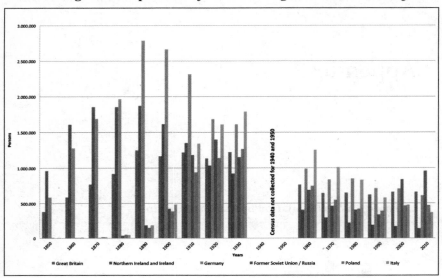

Note: Census data not collected for 1940 and 1950. Prior to 1960, census data were published for only a small number of countries outside of Europe, reflecting the small number of non-European countries which were numerically important sources of immigration to the United States.

Source: Gibson and Jung 2006b, Tables 3 and 4; Haines 2006a, Table Ad354-44; Haines 2006b, Table Aa1-5; 2010 American Community Survey.

178

US Foreign-Born Population by Nation of Origin: 1850-2010 – Asia

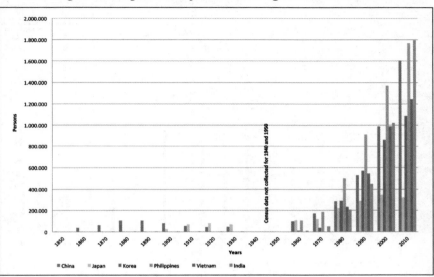

Note: Census data not collected for 1940 and 1950. Prior to 1960, census data were published for only a small number of countries outside of Europe, reflecting the small number of non-European countries which were numerically important sources of immigration to the United States.

Source: Gibson and Jung 2006b, Tables 3 and 4; Haines 2006a, Table Ad354-44; Haines 2006b, Table Aa1-5; 2010 American Community Survey.

US Foreign-Born Population by Nation of Origin 1850-2010 – Americas

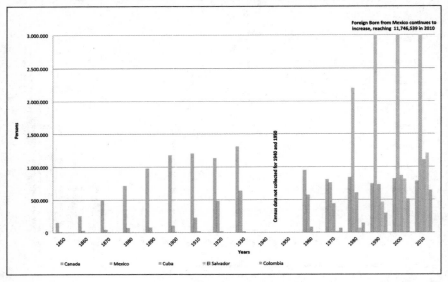

Note: Census data not collected for 1940 and 1950. Prior to 1960, census data were published for only a small number of countries outside of Europe, reflecting the small number of non-European countries which were numerically important sources of immigration to the United States.

Source: Gibson and Jung 2006b, Tables 3 and 4; Haines 2006a, Table Ad354-44; Haines 2006b, Table Aa1-5; 2010 American Community Survey.

Appendix B
Acronyms

ACCU	Association of Catholic Colleges and Universities
ACTU	Association of Catholic Trade Unionists
AFL-CIO	American Federation of Labor and Congress of Industrial Organizations
CARA	Center for Applied Research in the Apostolate
CCHD	Catholic Campaign for Human Development
CCUSA	Catholic Charities USA
CEF	Catholic Education Foundation
CELAM	Consejo Episcopal Latinoamericano
CHA	Catholic Health Association of the United States
CLINIC	Catholic Legal Immigration Network, Inc.
CLUE	Clergy and Laity United for Economic Justice
CMS	Center for Migration Studies of New York
DACA	Deferred Action for Childhood Arrivals
DHS	US Department of Homeland Security
DHS-CBP	US Department of Homeland Security, Customs and Border Protection
DREAM Act	Development, Relief, and Education for Alien Minors Act
ESL	English-as-a-Second Language
EU	European Union
GED	General Education Diploma
IBCO	Institution-Based Community Organization
IRCA	Immigration Reform and Control Act of 1986
IRS	Internal Revenue Service

LPR	Lawful Permanent Resident
MAA	Mutual Assistance Agency
MRS	USCCB Office of Migration and Refugee Services
NCCB	National Conference of Catholic Bishops
NCCC	National Conference of Catholic Charities
NCWC	National Catholic Welfare Council
PICO	Pacific Institute for Community Organization
PRRI	Public Religion Research Institute
USCCB	United States Conference of Catholic Bishops
SAD	United States Bishops' Social Action Department
USCC	United States Catholic Conference

References

ACCU (Association of Catholic Colleges and Universities). 2014. "Immigration Reform and Catholic Higher Education." http://www.accunet.org/i4a/pages/index.cfm?pageid=3781.

Alba, Richard, and Nancy Foner. 2014. "Comparing Immigrant Integration in North America and Western Europe: How Much Do the Grand Narratives Tell Us?" *International Migration Review* 48: S263-91.

Alba, Richard, Philip Kasinitz, and Mary C. Walters. 2011. "The Kids Are (Mostly) Alright: Second Generation Assimilation." *Social Forces* 89(3): 763-74.

Alba Richard, and Robert Orsi. 2009. "Passages in Piety: Generational Transitions and the Social and Religious Incorporation of Italian Americans." In *Immigration and Religion in America: Comparative and Historical Perspectives*, edited by Richard Alba, Albert J. Raboteau and Josh DeWind. New York: New York University Press.

Anti-Defamation League. 2008. *Immigrants Targeted: Extremist Rhetoric Moves into the Mainstream.* http://www.adl.org/assets/pdf/civil-rights/immigration/Immigrants-Targeted-UPDATE_2008.pdf.

Appleby, J. Kevin. 2013. "Moving Forward: Next Steps toward Immigration Reform." In *On 'Strangers No Longer': Perspectives on the Historic US-Mexican Catholic Bishops' Pastoral Letter on Migration*, edited by Todd Scribner and J. Kevin Appleby. Mahwah, NJ: Paulist Press.

Baker, Kimball. 2010. *Go to the Worker.* Milwaukee, Wisconsin: Marquette Press.

Barna: Hipanics. 2013. "The Longer Hispanics Experience US Culture, the Less Socially Conservative They Become." Barna Group. August 20.

http://hispanics.barna.org/the-longer-hispanics-experience-u-s-culture-the-less-socially-conservative-they-become/.

Bouche, Maryann. 2012. "Daughters of Charity Leaving Archdiocese." *Catholic Herald Online,* August 9. http://chnonline.org/news/local/11407-daughters-of-charity-leaving-archdiocese.html.

Broughman, Stephen P., Nancy L. Swaim, and Cassie A. Hryczaniuk. 2011. *Characteristics of Private Schools in the United States: Results from the 2009-10 Private School Universe Survey.* Washington, DC: US Department of Education (DOE), National Center for Education Statistics (NCES). http://nces.ed.gov/pubs2011/2011339.pdf.

Brown, Dorothy, M. and Elizabeth McKeown. 1997. *The Poor Belong to Us: Catholic Charities and American Welfare.* Cambridge, MA: Harvard University Press.

Brown, Susan K., and Frank D. Bean. 2006. "Assimilation Models, Old and New: Explaining a Long-Term Process." *Migration Information Source,* October 1. Washington, DC: Migration Policy Institute. http://www.migrationinformation.org/feature/display.cfm?id=442.

Bruce, Tricia C. 2006. "Contested Accommodation on the Meso Level: Discursive Adaptation Within Catholic Charities' Immigration and Refugee Services." *American Behavioral Scientist* 49 (11): 1489-1508.

Butler, Anne M. 2012. *Across God's Frontiers: Catholic Sisters in the American West, 1850-1920.* Chapel Hill, NC: University of North Carolina Press.

CARA (Center for Applied Research in the Apostolate). 2013. "Frequently Requested Church Statistics." Washington, DC: CARA. http://cara.georgetown.edu/CARAServices/requestedchurchstats.html.

Castelli, Jim. 1996. "How the Church Passes the Buck to the Poor." *US Catholic* 61(10): 21-26).

Cattaro, Gerald M. 2002. "Immigration and Pluralism in Urban Catholic Schools." *Education and Urban Society* 34(2): 199-211.

CCUSA (Catholic Charities USA). 2005. *Justice for Newcomers: A Catholic Call for Solidarity and Reform: Catholic Charities 2005 Policy Paper.* Alexandria, VA: Catholic Charities USA.

———.2014. *Help and Hope Report 2014: A Summary of the 2013 Annual Survey.* Alexandria, VA: Catholic Charities USA. https://www.scribd.com/doc/239814913/2014-Help-and-Hope-Report.

CEF (Catholic Education Foundation of Los Angeles). 2013. *Annual Report 2013.* Los Angeles, CA: Catholic Education Foundation of Los Angeles. http://www.cefdn.org/financials.

184

CELAM (Consejo Episcopal Latinoamericano). 2007. Concluding Document of the Fifth General Conference Fifth General Conference of the Latin American and Caribbean Bishops' Conferences, also known as "The Aparecida Document." http://www.celam.org/aparecida/Ingles.pdf.

CHA (Catholic Health Association). 2013a. "Catholic Identity." St. Louis, MO: Catholic Health Association. http://www.chausa.org/catholicidentity/overview.

———. 2013b. "Catholic Health Care in the United States." St. Louis, MO: Catholic Health Association. http://www.chausa.org/docs/default-source/general-files/mini_profile-pdf.pdf?sfvrsn=0.

Chamie, Joseph. 2014. "International Migration Trends and Perspectives for the United States of America." In *International Migration, US Immigration Law and Civil Society: From the Pre-Colonial Era to the 113th Congress*, edited by Donald Kerwin and Leonir Chiarello, C.S. New York: Scalabrini International Migration Network.

Christiansen, Drew. 1996. "Movement, Asylum, Borders: Christian Perspectives." *International Migration Review* 30(1): 7-17.

CLINIC (Catholic Legal Immigration Network, Inc.). 2000. *Work without Justice: Low-Wage Immigrant Laborers*. Washington, DC: Catholic Legal Immigration Network, Inc. http://www.ilw.com/articles/2005,1031-clinic.pdf.

Connor, Phillip, and Matthias Koenig. 2013. "Bridges and Barriers: Religion and Immigration Occupational Attainment across Integration Contexts." *International Migration Review* 47(1): 3-38.

Crawford, Mark. 2014. "Doctors from Abroad: A Cure for the Physician Shortage in America." *Health Progress* 95 (2): 45-48.

Day, Dorothy. 1934. "Christmas." *The Catholic Worker*, December 4. http://dorothyday.catholicworker.org/articles/199.html.

———. 1946. "Love is the Measure." *The Catholic Worker*, June, 2. http://www.catholicworker.org/dorothyday/daytext.cfm?TextID=425&SearchTerm=poor.

Deck, Allan F. 2013. "Pastoral Perspectives on Migration: Immigrants as New Evangelizers." In *On 'Strangers No Longer': Perspectives on the Historic US-Mexican Catholic Bishops' Pastoral Letter on Migration*, edited by Todd Scribner and J. Kevin Appleby. Mahwah, NJ: Paulist Press.

DHS (US Department of Homeland Security). 2012. *Yearbook of Immigration Statistics*. DHS Office of Immigration Statistics: Washington, DC.

https://www.dhs.gov/yearbook-immigration-statistics-2012-legal-permanent-residents.

DHS-CBP (US Department of Homeland Security, Customs and Border Protection). 2014. "Southwest Border Unaccompanied Alien Children." http://www.cbp.gov/newsroom/stats/southwest-border-unaccompanied-children.

Dias, Elizabeth. 2013. "The Rise of Evangélicos." *Time*, April 15, 22.

DiMarzio, Bishop Nicholas. 2014. "Integration of New Immigrants into US Catholic Church." *Origins* 43(40): 650-53.

Dolan, Jay P. 1992. *The American Catholic Experience: A History from Colonial Times to the Present*. Garden City, NY: Doubleday.

Dolan, His Eminence Timothy. 2014. "Learning Curve: How one archdiocese adapted its Catholic schools for the 21st century." *America*, October 20, 25.

Dominican University. 2012. "DU's Support for Undocumented Students a Moral Imperative." *Dominican* Fall. http://newsroom.dom.edu/sites/default/files/magazine/downloads/2012_fall_magazine.pdf.

Eby, Jessica, Erika Iverson, Jenifer Smyers and Erol Kekic. 2011. "The Faith Community's Role in Refugee Resettlement in the United States." *Journal of Refugee Studies* 24(3): 586-605.

Ellis, John T. 1955. "American Catholics and the Intellectual Life." *Thought* 30: 351-388. http://www.bc.edu/content/dam/files/offices/mission/pdf1/cu25.pdf.

Engel, Lawrence J. 1998. "The Influence of Saul Alinsky on the Campaign for Human Development." *Theological Studies* 59 (4): 636-61.

European Union. 2004. "Common Basic Principles for Immigrant Integration Policy in the European Union." European Commission Website on Integration. http://ec.europa.eu/ewsi/en/EU_actions_integration.cfm.

Fanning, William. 1908. "Archdiocese of New Orleans." *The Catholic Encyclopedia*. New York: Robert Appleton Company. http://www.newadvent.org/cathen/11005b.htm.

Farren, Suzy. 1996. *A Call to Care: The Women Who Built Catholic Healthcare in America*. St. Louis, MO and Washington, DC: The Catholic Health Association.

Fine, Janice. 2005. "Worker Centers: Organizing Communities at the Edge of the Dream." Briefing Paper. Washington, DC: Economic Policy Institute. http://www.epi.org/page/-/old/briefingpapers/159/bp159.pdf.

Finke, Roger and Rodney Stark. 1954. *The Churching of America, 1776-2005.* New Brunswick, NJ: Rutgers University Press.

Fisher, James T. 2008. *Communion of Immigrants: A History of Catholics in America.* New York: Oxford University Press.

Fitzpatrick, Joseph P. 1987. *One Church Many Cultures: The Challenge of Diversity.* Kansas City, MO: Sheed & Ward.

———. 1990. "Catholic Responses to Hispanic Newcomers." *Sociological Focus* 23(3): 155-66.

Foley, Michael W., and Dean R. Hoge. 2007. *Religion and the New Immigrants: How Faith Communities Form our Newest Citizens.* New York, NY: Oxford University Press.

Foner, Nancy, and Richard Alba. 2008. "Immigrant Religion in the US and Western Europe: Bridge or Barrier to Inclusion." *International Migration Review* 42(2): 360-92.

Galbraith, John K. 1979. *The Nature of Mass Poverty.* Cambridge, MA: Harvard University Press.

Gautier, Mary L., and C. Joseph O'Hara. 2012. *Catholic Charities USA 2011 Annual Survey Final Report.* Washington, DC: CARA.

Gerschutz, Jill M., with Lois A. Lorentzen. 2009. "Integration Yesterday and Today: New Challenges for the United States and the Church." In *And You Welcomed Me: Migration and Catholic Social Teaching,* edited by Donald Kerwin and Jill Gerschutz. Lanham, MD: Lexington Books.

Gibson, Campbell and Kay Yung. 2006a. *Historical Census Statistics on the Foreign-Born Population of the United States: 1850-2000.* Population Division Working Paper No. 29. Washington, DC: US Census Bureau.

———. 2006b. *Historical Census Statistics on the Foreign-Born Population of the United States: 1850-2000.* Population Division Working Paper No. 81. Washington, DC: US Census Bureau. http://www.census.gov/population/www/documentation/twps0081/twps0081.html.

Gleason, Philip. 1964. "Immigration and American Catholic Intellectual Life." *The Review of Politics* 26(2): 147-73.

Gray, Mark M., Melissa A. Cidade, Mary L. Gautier, and Thomas Gaunt, S. J. 2013. "Cultural Diversity in the Catholic Church in the United States." Washington, DC: CARA. http://www.usccb.org/issues-and-action/cultural-diversity/upload/cultural-diversity-cara-report-phase-1.pdf.

Gray, Mark M., Mary L. Gautier and Melissa A. Cidade. 2011. "The Changing Face of US Catholic Parishes." Washington DC: CARA. http://emergingmodels.org/wp-content/uploads/2012/04/Changing-Face-of-US-Catholic-Parishes.pdf.

———. 2013. "Views from the Pews: Parishioner Evaluations of Parish Life in the United States." Washington, DC: National Association for Lay Ministry. http://cara.georgetown.edu/staff/webpages/Parishioners%20Phase%20Three.pdf.

Greeley, Andrew M. 1962. "Anti-Intellectualism in Catholic Colleges." *American Catholic Sociological Review* 23: 350-68.

Grieco, Elizabeth M., Yesenia D. Acosta, G. Patricia de la Cruz, Christine Gambino, Thomas Gryn, Luke J. Larsen, Edward N. Trevelyan, and Nathan P. Walters. 2012. "The Foreign-Born Population in the United States: 2010." Washington, DC: United States Census Bureau. http://www.census.gov/prod/2012pubs/acs-19.pdf.

Groody, Daniel G. 2002. *Border of Death, Valley of Life: An Immigrant Journey of Heart and Spirit.* Lanham, MD: Rowman and Littlefield Press.

Hagan, Jacqueline. 2006. "Making Theological Sense of the Migration Journey from Latin America: Catholic, Protestant, and Interfaith Perspectives." *American Behavioral Scientist* 49(11): 1554-73.

Haines, Michael R. 2006a. "Foreign-born Population, by Country of Birth: 1850–1990." In *Historical Statistics of the United States, Earliest Times to the Present: Millennial Edition,* edited by Susan B. Carter, Scott Sigmund Gartner, Michael R. Haines, Alan L. Olmstead, Richard Sutch, and Gavin Wright. New York: Cambridge University Press. http://dx.doi.org/10.1017/ISBN-9780511132971.Ad256-949.

———. 2006b. "Population, Population Density, and Land Area: 1790-2000 [Original counts for census dates]." In *Historical Statistics of the United States, Earliest Times to the Present: Millennial Edition,* edited by Susan B. Carter, Scott Sigmund Gartner, Michael R. Haines, Alan L. Olmstead, Richard Sutch, and Gavin Wright. New York: Cambridge University Press.

Haller, William, Alejandro Portes, and Scott M. Lynch. 2011. "Dreams Fulfilled, Dreams Shattered: Determinants of Segmented Assimilation in the Second Generation." *Social Forces* 89(3): 733-62.

Hassenger, Robert. 1969. "Conflict in Catholic Colleges." *Annals of the American Academy of Political and Social Science* 382: 95-108.

Higareda, Ignacio, Shane P. Martin, Jose M. Chavez, and Karen Holyk-Casey. 2011. "Los Angeles Catholic Schools: Impact and Opportunity for Economically Disadvantaged Students." Los Angeles, CA: Loyola Marymount University, School of Education. http://soe.lmu.edu/media/

lmuschoolofeducation/departments/cce/contentassets/documents/ LMU%20Catholic%20School%20Research%20Project%20Phase%20 2%20Report.pdf.

Higgins, Monsignor George G., with William Bole. 1993. *Organized Labor and the Church*. Mahwah, NJ: Paulist Press.

Himes, Rev. Kenneth, OFM. 1996. "The Rights of People Regarding Migration: A Perspective from Catholic Social Teaching." *Who Are My Sisters and Brothers: Reflections on Understanding and Welcoming Immigrants and Refugees*, edited by Suzanne Hall. Washington, DC: United States Catholic Conference.

Hoffer, Thomas, Andrew M. Greeley, and James S. Coleman. 1985. "Achievement Growth in Public and Catholic Schools." *Sociology of Education* 58(2): 74-97.

Hoover, Brett. 2014. *The Shared Parish: Latinos, Anglos and the Future of US Catholicism*. New York: New York University Press.

Huchting, Karen K., Shane P. Martin, Jose M. Chavez, Karen Holyk-Casey, and Delmy Ruiz. 2014. *Los Angeles Catholic Schools: Academic Excellence and Character Formation for Students Living in Poverty*. LMU Catholic Schools Research Project Phase Three, Center for Catholic Education. Los Angeles, CA: Loyola Marymount University School of Education. http://soe.lmu.edu/media/lmuschoolofeducation/contentassets/ documents/LMU%20Los%20Angeles%20Catholic%20Schools%20 Phase%203-Report.pdf.

Huddleston, T., and Jan Niessen, with Eadaoin Ni Chaoimh and Emilie White. 2011. *Migrant Integration Policy Index III*. Brussels: British Council and Migration Policy Group. www.mipex.eu.

Jiménez, Tomás R. 2011. "Immigrants in the United States: How Well Are They Integrating into Society?" Wahsington, DC: Migration Policy Institute. http://www.migrationpolicy.org/pubs/integration-jimenez.pdf.

Johnson, Mary, Patricia Wittberg and Mary Gautier. 2014. *New Generations of Catholic Sisters: The Challenge of Diversity*. New York: Oxford University Press.

Johnson-Mondragón, Ken. 2008. "Ministry in Multicultural and National/ Ethnic Parishes: Evaluating the Findings of the Emerging Models of Pastoral Leadership Project." Stockton, CA: Instituto Fe y Vida. http://www. faithformationlearningexchange.net/uploads/5/2/4/6/5246709/multicultural_report_-_emerging_models_project.pdf.

Kauffman, Christopher J. 1995. *Ministry and Meaning: A Religious History of Catholic Health Care in the United States.* New York: The Crossroad Publishing Company.

Kaneb, Bruce, Brandy Ellison, and Jeyson Florez. 2010. "ACE Consulting Report to Support Efforts to Recruit Latino Students for the Diocese of Brooklyn." Notre Dame, IN: Alliance for Catholic Education, University of Notre Dame.

Kerwin, Donald. 2009a. "Toward a Catholic Vision of Nationality." *Notre Dame Journal of Law, Ethics & Public Policy* 23(a): 197-207.

———. 2009b. "Rights, the Common Good, and Sovereignty in Service of the Human Person." In *And You Welcomed Me: Migration and Catholic Social Teaching,* edited by Donald Kerwin and Jill Gerschutz. Lanham, MD: Lexington Books.

———. 2012. "The Faltering US Refugee Protection System: Legal and Policy Responses to Refugees, Asylum Seekers, and Others in Need of Protection." *Refugee Survey Quarterly* 31(1): 1-33.

———. 2013a. "Sovereignty in Service to Human Security." In *Safe International Migration: Proceedings of the Second and Third International Forums on Migration and Peace,* edited by Leonir M. Chiarello. New York: Scalabrini International Migration Network.

———. 2013b. "The US Labor Standards Enforcement System and Low-Wage Immigrants: Recommendations for Legislative and Administrative Reforms." *Journal on Migration and Human Security* 1: 32-57.

———. 2013c. "Migration, Development, and the Right Not to Have to Migrate in the New Era of Globalization." In *On 'Strangers No Longer': Perspectives on the Historic US-Mexican Catholic Bishops' Pastoral Letter on Migration,* edited by Todd Scribner and J. Kevin Appleby. Mahwah, NJ: Paulist Press.

Louie, Vivian, and Jennifer Holdaway. 2009. "Catholic Schools and Immigrant Students: A New Generation." *Teachers College Record* 111(3): 783-816.

Marks, Jessica A. 2014. "Rural Refugee Resettlement: Secondary Migration and Community Integration in Fort Morgan, Colorado." New Issues in Refugee Research, Research Paper No. 269. Geneva: UNHCR Policy Development and Evaluation Service. http://www.unhcr.org/5326c7cd9.html.

Matovina, Timothy. 2012. *Latino Catholicism: Transformation in America's Largest Church.* Princeton, NJ: Princeton University Press.

McDonald, Dale, and Margaret M. Schultz. 2013. *United States Catholic Elementary and Secondary Schools 2012-2013: The Annual Statistical Report* on *Schools, Enrollment and Staffing*. Arlington, VA: National Catholic Educational Association.

McGreevy, John T. 2003. *Catholicism and American Freedom*. New York: W.W. Norton & Company.

McShane, Joseph M. 1990. "'The Church is Not for the Cells and the Caves': The Working Class Spirituality of the Jesuit Labor Priests." *US Catholic Historian* 9(3): 289-304.

Meissner, Doris, Donald Kerwin, Muzaffar Chishti, and Claire Bergeron. 2013. *Immigration Enforcement in the United States: The Rise of a Formidable Machinery*. Washington, DC: Migration Policy Institute. http://www.migrationpolicy.org/pubs/enforcementpillars.pdf.

Menjívar, Cecilia. 1999. "Religious Institutions and Transnationalism: A Case Study of Catholic and Evangelical Salvadoran Immigrants." *International Journal of Politics, Culture and Society* 12(4): 589-612.

———. 2003. "Religion and Immigration in Comparative Perspective: Catholic and Evangelical Salvadorans in San Francisco, Washington, DC, and Phoenix." *Sociology of Religion* 64(1): 21-45.

Miner, Brad. 2013. "Why the Catholic Bishops Are Wrong on Immigration." *The Catholic Thing*. July 29. http://www.thecatholicthing.org/columns/2013/why-the-bishops-are-wrong-on-immigration.html.

Mooney, Margarita. 2007. "The Catholic Church's Institutional Responses to Immigration: From Supranational to Local Engagement." In *Religion and Social Justice for Immigrants*, edited by Pierrette Hondagneu-Sotelo. New Brunswick, NJ: Rutgers University Press.

Morris, Charles R. 1997. *American Catholic: The Saints and Sinners Who Build America's Most Powerful Church*. New York: Vintage Books.

Morrison, James L., and Benjamin J. Hodgkins. 1971. "The Effectiveness of Catholic Education: A Comparative Analysis." *Sociology of Education* 44(1): 119-131.

Motel, Seth, and Eileen Patten. 2013. "Statistical Portrait of the Foreign-Born Population in the United States, 2011." Washington, DC: Pew Hispanic Center. http://www.pewhispanic.org/2013/01/29/statistical-portrait-of-the-foreign-born-population-in-the-united-states-2011/.

Myers, Dowell, and John Pitkin. 2011. *Assimilation Tomorrow: How America's Immigrants Will Integrate by 2030*. Washington, DC: Center for American Progress. http://cdn.americanprogress.org/wp-content/uploads/issues/2011/11/pdf/dowell_assimilation_report.pdf.

Nawyn, Stephanie J. 2006. "Faith, Ethnicity, and Culture in Refugee Resettlement." *American Behavioral Scientist* 49(11): 1509-27.

National Catholic War Council, Administrative Committee. 1919. "Bishops' Program for Social Reconstruction." http://www.stthomas.edu/cath-studies/cst/aboutus/bishopsprogram.html.

NCCB (National Conference of Catholic Bishops). 1986. *Together a New People: Pastoral Statement on Migrants and Refugees.* Washington, DC: NCCB.

NCES (National Center for Educational Statistics). 1993. *120 Years of American Education: A Statistical Portrait.* Edited by Thomas D. Snyder. Washington, DC: National Center for Educational Statistics. http://nces.ed.gov/pubs93/93442.pdf

North, David. 2011. "The 'One-Off' Migrants: A Proposed Fantasy Immigration Policy." Washington, DC: Center for Immigration Studies. http://www.cis.org/north/one-off-migrants

Notre Dame Task Force on the Participation of Latina Children and Families in Catholic Schools. 2009. *To Nurture the Soul of a Nation: Latino(a) Families, Catholic Schools, and Educational Opportunity.* Notre Dame, IN: Alliance for Catholic Education Press. http://ace.nd.edu/files/ACE-CSA/nd_ltf_report_final_english_12.2.pdf

Oates, Mary J. 1995. *The Catholic Philanthropic Tradition in America.* Bloomington and Indianapolis, IN: Indiana University Press.

Odem, Mary E. 2004. "Our Lady of Guadalupe in the New South: Latino Immigrants and the Politics of Integration in the Catholic Church." *Journal on American Ethnic History* 24(1): 26-57.

Ospino, Hosffman. 2014a. *Hispanic Ministry in Catholic Parishes: A Summary Report of Findings from the "National Study of Catholic Parishes with Hispanic Ministry.* Boston, MA: Boston College School of Theology and Ministry. http://www.bc.edu/content/dam/files/schools/stm/pdf/2014/HispanicMinistryinCatholicParishes_2.pdf.

———. 2014b. "Integration of Latino Immigrants in Catholic Parishes: A Few Emerging Insights from the 2011-2013 National Study of Catholic Parishes with Hispanic Ministry." Presentation at Center for Migration Studies' Conference on Immigrant Integration, February 24. http://cmsny.org/programs/catholicintegration/.

Ottonelli, Valeria, and Tiziana Torresi. 2013. "When is Migration Voluntary?" *International Migration Review* 47(4): 783-813.

Pastor, Manuel, Rhonda Ortiz, Vanessa Carter, Justin Scoggins, and Anthony Perez. 2012. *California Immigrant Integration Scorecard.* Los

Angeles, CA: University of Southern California, Center for Study of Immigrant Integration. http://csii.usc.edu/documents/California_ Immigrant_Integration_Scorecard_web.pdf.

The Pew Forum on Religion and Public Life and the Pew Hispanic Center. 2007. *Changing Faiths: Latino(a)s and the Transformation of American Religion*. Washington, DC: Pew Research Center. http://www.pew-forum.org/uploadedfiles/Topics/Demographics/hispanics-religion-07-final-mar08.pdf.

The Pew Forum on Religion and Public Life. 2008. *US Religious Landscape Survey: Religious Affiliation: Diverse and Dynamic*. Washington, DC: The Pew Forum on Religion & Public Life. http://religions.pewforum. org/pdf/report-religious-landscape-study-full.pdf.

Pew Research Center. 2014. *The Shifting Religious Identity of Latinos in the United States: Nearly One-in-Four Latinos Are Former Catholics*. http:// www.pewforum.org/files/2014/05/Latinos-and-Religion-05-06-full-report-final.pdf.

P.J. Kenedy & Sons. *The Official Catholic Directory*, 1910-2010 vols.

Pontifical Council for Justice and Peace. 2005. *Compendium of the Social Doctrine of the Church*. http://www.vatican.va/roman_curia/pontifical_ councils/justpeace/documents/rc_pc_justpeace_doc_20060526_ compendio-dott-soc_en.html.

———. 2012. *Vocation of the Business Leader: A Reflection*. http://www.pcgp. it/dati/2012-05/04-999999/Vocation%20ENG2.pdf.

Pontifical Council for the Pastoral Care of Migrants and Itinerant People. 2004. *Erga migrantes caritas Christi (The love of Christ towards migrants)*. http://www.vatican.va/roman_curia/pontifical_councils/mi-grants/documents/rc_pc_migrants_doc_20040514_erga-migrant-es-caritas-christi_en.html.

Pope Benedict XVI. 2005. *Deus Caritas Est (God is Love)*. http://www.vatican. va/holy_father/benedict_xvi/encyclicals/documents/hf_ben-xvi_ enc_20051225_deus-caritas-est_en.html.

———. 2009. *Caritas in Veritate (On Integral Human Development in Charity and Truth)*. http://www.vatican.va/holy_father/benedict_xvi/encyc-licals/documents/hf_ben-xvi_enc_20090629_caritas-in-veritate_ en.html.

———. 2011. *Message of His Holiness Benedict XVI for the 97th World Day of Migrants and Refugees*. http://www.vatican.va/holy_father/benedict_ xvi/messages/migration/documents/hf_ben-xvi_mes_20100927_ world-migrants-day_en.html.

Pope Francis. 2013a. *Lumen Fidei (The Light of Faith)*. http://www.vatican.va/holy_father/francesco/encyclicals/documents/papa-francesco_20130629_enciclica-lumen-fidei_en.html.

_____. 2013b. *Evangelii Gaudium (The Joy of the Gospel)*. http://w2.vatican.va/content/francesco/en/apost_exhortations/documents/papa-francesco_esortazione-ap_20131124_evangelii-gaudium.html.

———. 2014. *Message of His Holiness Pope Francis for the World Day of Migrants and Refugees: Towards a Better World.* http://www.vatican.va/holy_father/francesco/messages/migration/documents/papa-francesco_20130805_world-migrants-day_en.html.

Pope John Paul II. 1975. *Evangelii Nuntiandi (On Evangelization in the Modern World)*. http://www.papalencyclicals.net/Paul06/p6evan.htm.

———. 1995. *Ut Unum Sint (On Commitment to Ecumenism)*. http://www.vatican.va/holy_father/john_paul_ii/encyclicals/documents/hf_jp-ii_enc_25051995_ut-unum-sint_en.html.

———. 1999. Post-Synodal Apostolic Exhortation, *Ecclesia in America (The Church in America)*. http://www.vatican.va/holy_father/john_paul_ii/apost_exhortations/documents/hf_jp-ii_exh_22011999_ecclesia-in-america_en.html.

_____. 2001. *Message of His Holiness Pope John Paul II for the Celebration of the World Day of Peace.* http://www.vatican.va/holy_father/john_paul_ii/messages/peace/documents/hf_jp-ii_mes_20001208_xxxiv-world-day-for-peace_en.html.

Pope Leo XIII. 1891. *Rerum Novarum (On Capital and Labor)*. In *The Papal Encyclicals 1878-1903*, edited by Claudia Carlen, IHM. Raleigh, NC: McGrath Publishing Company.

Pope Paul VI. 1964. Dogmatic Constitution on the Church, *Lumen Gentium (Light of the World)*. http://www.vatican.va/archive/hist_councils/ii_vatican_council/documents/vat-ii_const_19641121_lumen-gentium_en.html.

———. 1965. Pastoral Constitution on the Church in the Modern World, *Gaudium et Spes (Hope and Joy)*. http://www.vatican.va/archive/hist_councils/ii_vatican_council/documents/vat-ii_cons_19651207_gaudium-et-spes_en.html.

———. 1967. *Populorum Progressio (On the Development of Peoples)*. http://www.vatican.va/holy_father/paul_vi/encyclicals/documents/hf_p-vi_enc_26031967_populorum_en.html.

Pope Pius XI. 1931. *Quadragesimo Anno (On Reconstruction of the Social*

RERENCES

Order). In *The Papal Encyclicals 1903-1939,* edited by Claudia Carlen, IHM. Raleigh, NC: McGrath Publishing Company.

Portes, Alejandro, and Min Zhou. 1993. "The New Second Generation: Segmented Assimilation and Its Variants." *The Annals of the American Academy of Political and Social Sciences* 530(1): 74-96.

PRRI (Public Religion Research Institute/Brookings Institution). 2013. *Religion Values, and Immigration Reform Survey.*

Putnam, Robert D., and David E. Campbell. 2010. *American Grace: How Religion Divides and Unites Us.* New York: Simon & Schuster.

Robles, Gabriela, Verónica F. Gutiérrez, and George B. Avila. 2014. "Supporting the Newest Among Our Dear Neighbors: How One Health System Helps Immigrants to Thrive." *Health Progress* 95 (2): 18-23.

Ruhs, Martin. 2013. *The Price of Rights: Regulating International Labor Migration.* Princeton, NJ: Princeton University Press.

Ryscavage, Richard. 2012. "Open Doors to Immigrants." *America* 207(12): 15.

Sagarena, Roberto L. 2009. "Migration and Mexican American Religious Life, 1848-2000." In *Immigration and Religion in America: Comparative and Historical Perspectives,* edited by Richard Alba, Albert J. Raboteau and Josh DeWind. New York: New York University Press.

Schlichting, Kurt, Terry-Ann Jones, Suzanna Klaf, Philip Nyden, Maria Guzman, Laura Nichols, Ana Siscar, Mary Bird, and Cynthia Mertens. 2013. "Immigrant Student National Position Paper Report on Findings: Executive Summary." Fairfield, CT: Fairfield University. http://www.fairfield.edu/documents/academic/cfpl_immigration_report.pdf.

Scribner, Todd. 2010. "Negotiating Priorities: The National Catholic Welfare Conference and United States Migration Policy in a Post-World War II World, 1948-1952." American Catholic Studies 121(4): 1-25.

———. Forthcoming. "'Not Because They Are Catholic, But Because We Are Catholic': The Catholic Bishops Engage The Migration Issue In Twentieth Century America." *The Catholic Historical Review.*

Shaughnessy, Gerald. 1925. *Has the Immigrant Kept the Faith? A Study of Immigration and Catholic Growth in the United States.* New York: Macmillan Co.

Simansky, John F., and Lesley M. Sapp. 2013. "Immigration Enforcement Actions 2012." Washington, DC: DHS Office of Immigration Statistics. http://www.dhs.gov/sites/default/files/publications/ois_enforcement_ar_2012_0.pdf.

Smarick, Andy. 2011. "Can Catholic Schools Be Saved?" *National Affairs* 1(7): 113-130. http://www.nationalaffairs.com/doclib/20110317_Smarick.pdf.

Smith, Timothy L. 1978. "Religion and Ethnicity in America." *American Historical Review* 83: 1155-85.

Snyder, Thomas D., and Sally A. Dillow. 2013. *Digest of Education Statistics 2012.* Washington, DC: Department of Education and National Center for Education Statistics. http://nces.ed.gov/pubs2014/2014015.pdf.

Stibili, Edward C. 2003. *What Can Be Done to Help Them?: The Italian Saint Raphael Society 1887-1923.* New York: Center for Migration Studies.

Stovski, Renee. 2014. "Bon Secours Links English Literacy and Parenting Skills Classes." St. Louis, MO: Catholic Health Association. https://www.chausa.org/publications/catholic-health-world/article/february-1-2014/bon-secours-links-english-literacy-and-parenting-skills-classes.

Third Plenary Council of Baltimore. 1884. "Pastoral Letter Issued by the Third Plenary Council of Baltimore." In *Pastoral Letters of the United States Catholic Bishop, Volume I 1792-1940*, edited by Hugh J. Nolan. Washington, DC: National Conference of Catholic Bishops/United States Catholic Conference.

Tomasi, Silvano M. 1975. *Piety and Power: The Role of Italian Parishes in the New York Metropolitan Area, 1880-1930.* New York: Center for Migration Studies.

United States Census Bureau. 2010 American Community Survey. Washington, DC: US Census Bureau. http://dataferrett.census.gov.

USCC (United States Catholic Conference). 1987. *National Pastoral Plan for Hispanic Ministry.* Washington, DC: United States Catholic Conference.

———. 2000. *Welcoming the Stranger Among Us: Unity in Diversity.* Washington, DC: United States Catholic Conference. http://www.usccb.org/issues-and-action/cultural-diversity/pastoral-care-of-migrants-refugees-and-travelers/resources/welcoming-the-stranger-among-us-unity-in-diversity.cfm.

USCCB (United States Conference of Catholic Bishops). 2002. *Encuentro and Mission: A Renewed Framework for Hispanic Ministry.* Washington, DC: United States Conference of Catholic Bishops. http://old.usccb.org/hispanicaffairs/encuentromission.shtml#2.

———. 2006. "A Labor Day Reflection on Immigration and Work." Washington, DC: United States Conference of Catholic Bishops. http://www.usccb.org/issues-and-action/human-life-and-dignity/labor-employment/upload/LaborDay2006.pdf.

———. 2008. African and Caribbean Catholics in the United States. Washington, DC: United States Conference of Catholic Bishops. http://www.usccb.org/issues-and-action/cultural-diversity/pastoral-care-of-migrants-refugees-and-travelers/ethnic-ministries/upload/ACC.pdf.

———. 2012. *Building Intercultural Competence for Ministers*. Washington, DC: United States Conference of Catholic Bishops.

United States Conference of Catholic Bishops and Conferencia del Episcopado Mexicano. 2003. *Strangers No Longer: Together on the Journey of Hope*. Washington, DC: United States Conference of Catholic Bishops. http://www.usccb.org/issues-and-action/human-life-and-dignity/immigration/strangers-no-longer-together-on-the-journey-of-hope.cfm.

Warren, Robert, and John Robert Warren. 2013. "Unauthorized Immigration to the United States: Annual Estimates and Components of Change, by State, 1990 to 2010." *International Migration Review* 47 (2): 296-329. http://onlinelibrary.wiley.com/doi/10.1111/imre.12022/pdf.

White, Kenneth R. 2000. "Hospitals Sponsored by the Roman Catholic Church: Separate, Equal, and Distinct?" *The Milbank Quarterly* 78 (2): 213-239.

Wood, Richard L., Brad Fulton, and Kathryn Partridge. 2012. *Building Bridges, Building Power: Developments in Institution-Based Community Organizing*. Longmont, Colorado: InterfaithFunders. http://www.soc.duke.edu/~brf6/ibcoreport.pdf.

Williams, Philip J., and Patricia Fortuny. 2013. "Looking for Lived Religion in Immokalee." In *A Place to Be: Identity, Transnationalism and Religion in the Sunshine State*. New Brunswick, NJ: Rutgers University Press.

Williams, Philip J., Manuel A. Vásquez, Timothy J. Steigenga, and Marie F. Marquardt. n.d. "Latin American Immigrants in the New South: Religion and the Politics of Encounter." Research Brief based on a Preliminary Report.

Table of Contents

Collana *Vivae voces*

1. R. Tremblay – S. Zamboni, *Ritrovarsi donandosi. Alcune idee chiave della teologia di Joseph Ratzinger-Benedetto XVI*

2. M. Cozzoli (ed.), *Pensare professare vivere la fede. Nel solco della lettera apostolica "Porta Fidei"*

3. C. L. Rossetti, *La pienezza di Cristo. Verità, comunione e adorazione. Saggio sulla cattolicità della Chiesa*

4. F. Felice – J. Spitzer (edd.), *Il Ruolo delle istituzioni alla luce dei principi di sussidiarietà, di poliarchia e di solidarietà. Atti del colloquio internazionale di Dottrina Sociale della Chiesa*

5. S. Lanza, *Opus Lateranum. Saggi di teologia pastorale*

6. S. Capodieci, *Giuseppe. Storia di fratellanza e amicizia. Psicologia e Bibbia in dialogo*

7. G. Battista, *Teologia dell'educazione cristiana: pluralità di modelli e di strategie. Un'antologia di testi*

8. S. Zamboni (ed.), *Etica dell'infanzia. Questioni aperte*

9. R. Tadiello – M. Bennati, *L'itineranza di Abramo nella difficile strada della rielaborazione del lutto. Psicologia e Bibbia in dialogo*

10. D. Petti, *Dialogo sulla politica con Papa Benedetto XVI*

11. N. Ciola, *Concilio Vaticano II e rinnovamento teologico*

12. A. Sabetta (ed.), *Fidei doctrinae fundamentum: veritas Evangelii per se ipsam praesens*

13. R. Swinburne, *Esiste un Dio? Nuova edizione*

14. E. dal Covolo, *Forme di vita spirituale nei Padri della Chiesa*

15. C. Cellini, *Ad alba inoltrata 1993 – 1985. Tutte le poesie*

16. A. Carollo, *Pietro e Gesù. Gli alti e i bassi della sequela*

17. F. Felice – A. Campati (edd.), *Se vuoi la pace costruisci istituzioni di pace. Atti del Colloquio Internazionale di Dottrina sociale della Chiesa*

18. N. Ciola – G. Ghiberti (edd.), *La Passione di Gesù e la Sindone*

19. A. Franzini, *Tradizione e scrittura. Il contributo del concilio Vaticano II*

20. S. Capodieci, *Re Salomone e il fenomeno dell'invidia. Psicologia e Bibbia in dialogo*

21. A. Buckenmaier – L. Weimer (edd.), *A Poor People of God for the Poor in the World? – The Challenge of Pope Francis*

22. G. Tangorra, *Temi di ecclesiologia*

23. L. Andreatta – C. Costa – P. Asolan (edd.), *Eucarestia Pane del pellegrino. 80° Opera Romana Pellegrinaggi 1934-2014*

24. M. Serretti, *Persona e anima*

25. F. Felice – G. Taiani (edd.), *Il denaro deve servire, non governare*

26. D. Kerwin, with B. George, *US Catholic Institutions and Immigrant Integration: Will the Church Rise to the Challenge?*